CHINESE STORIES
FOR LANGUAGE LEARNERS

ELEMENTARY

Chinese • Pinyin • English

LingLing

www.linglingmandarin.com

enquiries@linglingmandarin.com

FIRST EDITION

Editing by Xinrong Huo
Cover design by Ling Ling

www.linglingmandarin.com

My gratitude goes to my wonderful students who study Mandarin with me – you have inspired my writing and had given me valuable feedback to complete this book. Your support is deeply appreciated!

I would also like to thank Hua Hailing, Huo Xinrong, and Dai Zhiming for their contributions to the audio recordings.

Special thanks go to my husband Phil, who motivated my creation and assisted with the editing and proofreading of the book.

Access FREE AUDIO

Check the **"ACCESS AUDIO"** chapter for password and full instructions (see Table of Contents)

TABLE OF CONTENTS

INTRODUCTION

Are you tired of dull, uninspiring textbooks or struggling to maintain momentum and motivation to keep progressing in your Chinese learning journey? Reading broadly and extensively is key to building up vocabulary in Chinese, but it doesn't have to be boring! Do you also have an interest in authentic Chinese culture and a desire to deepen your understanding of the things that make Chinese people tick? If yes, then **congratulations, you have come to the right place!**

If you are ready to take the next step to level up your Chinese through fun and engaging stories while filling your Chinese-language toolbox with essential vocabulary and crucial sentence patterns, then read on and enjoy because this book will do just that and more! This book presents an entertaining and insightful approach to learning Chinese language and culture through stories!

We will explore myths and legends, proverbs and poetry, and much more from throughout China's long and rich history. Literature has always played a critical and influential part throughout Chinese history. Of course, there are contemporary stories set in the modern day as well! Each short story has been written and specially selected for elementary-level students. For those of you who enjoy narratives set in modern China, check out my book **Chinese Conversations for Beginners**.

Not only will you improve your Chinese with this book, but you will also get to know the origins of traditional Chinese festivals; discover valuable life lessons and wisdom from China's most notable classics; learn witty Chinese idioms and proverbs to impress your peers; and, gain powerful linguistic and cultural insights from both the stories themselves and the additional **learning tips** and **culture corners** along the way!

HOW THE BOOK WILL HELP

This book contains 25 stories with expanded learning content, written and selected for elementary-level students, with the length of each story between 200 – 400 words. Most stories are well-known Chinese classics that touch on a variety of topics and themes and selected from different areas of Chinese literature and culture, including:

- Chinese Myths
- Chinese Fables
- Modern Stories
- Chinese Idioms
- Chinese Folktales
- Chinese Proverbs
- Chinese Poetry with Love Stories

Each story is structured to guide and assist your learning while making your learning journey entertaining and memorable through:

- Bilingual story with Chinese, Pinyin, and English
- Chinese-only version of the story for self-assessment
- Key vocabulary list to help you to learn and review
- Sentence patterns with examples in context
- Activities or exercises to help you to reflect and remember
- Learning tips and culture corner to enhance your understanding
- FREE AUDIO recorded by native speakers

You will learn the original stories behind traditional Chinese festivals, like Chinese New Year, Mid-Autumn Festival, and the Qixi Festival (Chinese Valentine's Day). You will explore powerful and touching stories that helped to shape traditional Chinese values. You will discover ancient Chinese wisdom that is deeply embedded in Chinese culture. You will be entertained with amusing stories from modern China that will make you laugh and smile. You will also learn witty Chinese idioms and proverbs, which are short in form but deep in meaning and still used frequently in everyday life. Through these fun stories, you will get to know their origins and be able to use them to stand out from the crowd and impress your Chinese friends and peers, and, most importantly, speak with confidence!

As the focus of this book is to assist learners of modern Chinese, all words and vocabulary are purposely from contemporary vernacular. In some cases, such as ancient classics and historical stories, some words have been exchanged for modern equivalent. For example, the word “prime minister” was called “丞(chéng)相(xiàng)” in ancient Chinese, but in the book is referred to as “首(shǒu)相(xiàng)” to reflect the modern term.

FREE DOWNLOADABLE AUDIO

Great news! The audio files for the book are a FREE gift for you, my beloved readers, who purchase this book. The audio is all recorded by native speakers. Be sure to check the **Access Audio** page toward the end of hte book (see Table of Contents) for instructions on how to access; the page also contains the required password!

LEARN CHINESE WITH A NEW VISION

Chinese is one of the most varied, dynamic, and artistic languages and has developed over 3500 years. It is one of the most spoken languages in the world, and mastering it opens doors to new opportunities in life, travel, business, and personal development.

Studying Chinese is not just about learning a new language but also exploring a different way of thinking, experiencing new perspectives, understanding a rich culture developed over thousands of years, and finding peace and balance in a life-long beneficial journey.

LEARNING TIPS

BECOME AN EFFECTIVE LEARNER

In Chinese, we have a well-known idiom 事半功倍 (shì bàn gōng bèi) (get twice the result with half the effort). You can cut short a long process with an effective learning method. It may seem obvious, but the best way to learn Chinese is to use it as often as possible, especially with Chinese speaking and listening. The more you practice, the more it will become second nature, like muscle memory. But you need an excellent strategy to be effective.

Make the most of each story in the book by paying attention to the language flow and keep **reading it aloud** until you can read it naturally and fluently – even imagining yourself being the story teller. Use the accompanying audio to help by imitating the accent and expression of the people in the audio. I suggest you follow this process:

1. **Read** the bilingual version of each story to identify the new words and phrases in context, referring to the key vocabulary list and sentence patterns for usage.
2. **Listen** to the audio while following the text to pick up the correct pronunciation - pause and rewind if necessary.
3. **Practice** reading the text aloud until you can read the entire story fluently. Pay attention to transitional words and phrases to master the authentic language flow.
4. **Test** yourself by heading to the Chinese version of the story, and read it without the help of Pinyin and English. Mastering the Chinese on its own is the key to level up.
5. **Listen again** to the audio. Test yourself by listening to it without the help of the text. If you miss some parts, go back to check with the text. Keep practicing until you can comprehend the audio alone.

REVIEW AND PRACTICE

Repetition is the mother of learning! Make sure you go back to each story and review the vocabularies and sentence patterns frequently. The more you review and practice, the better your Mandarin will be!

BE YOUR OWN CREATOR

Become a true master through creation and application! Apply the vocabularies, phrases, and sentence patterns you learned from each story to your own conversations, whether in real-life practice or imaginary scenarios. Remember – the ultimate goal of learning Mandarin is to effectively communicate and understand the language in your own experiences. You can only achieve this by applying what you have learned in practice!

BELIEVE IN YOURSELF

Believe in yourself and have confidence! Never be afraid of making mistakes. In real life, even advanced learners and native speakers make mistakes! Plus, mistakes only make us grow quicker! So, never let mistakes put you off. Instead, be bold, embrace and learn from mistakes!

SET GOALS AND STAY COMMITTED

Having a committed learning attitude and setting goals from small to big will lead you to great achievements in your Chinese learning journey. So stay committed and never give up! Just like this Chinese idiom:

Nothing is Impossible to a Willing Heart

神 shén
话 huà
故 gù
事 shì

Chinese Myths

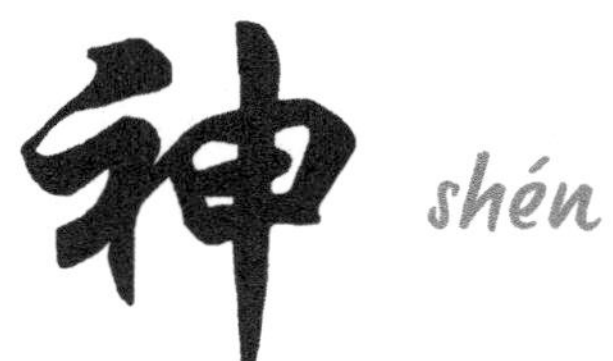

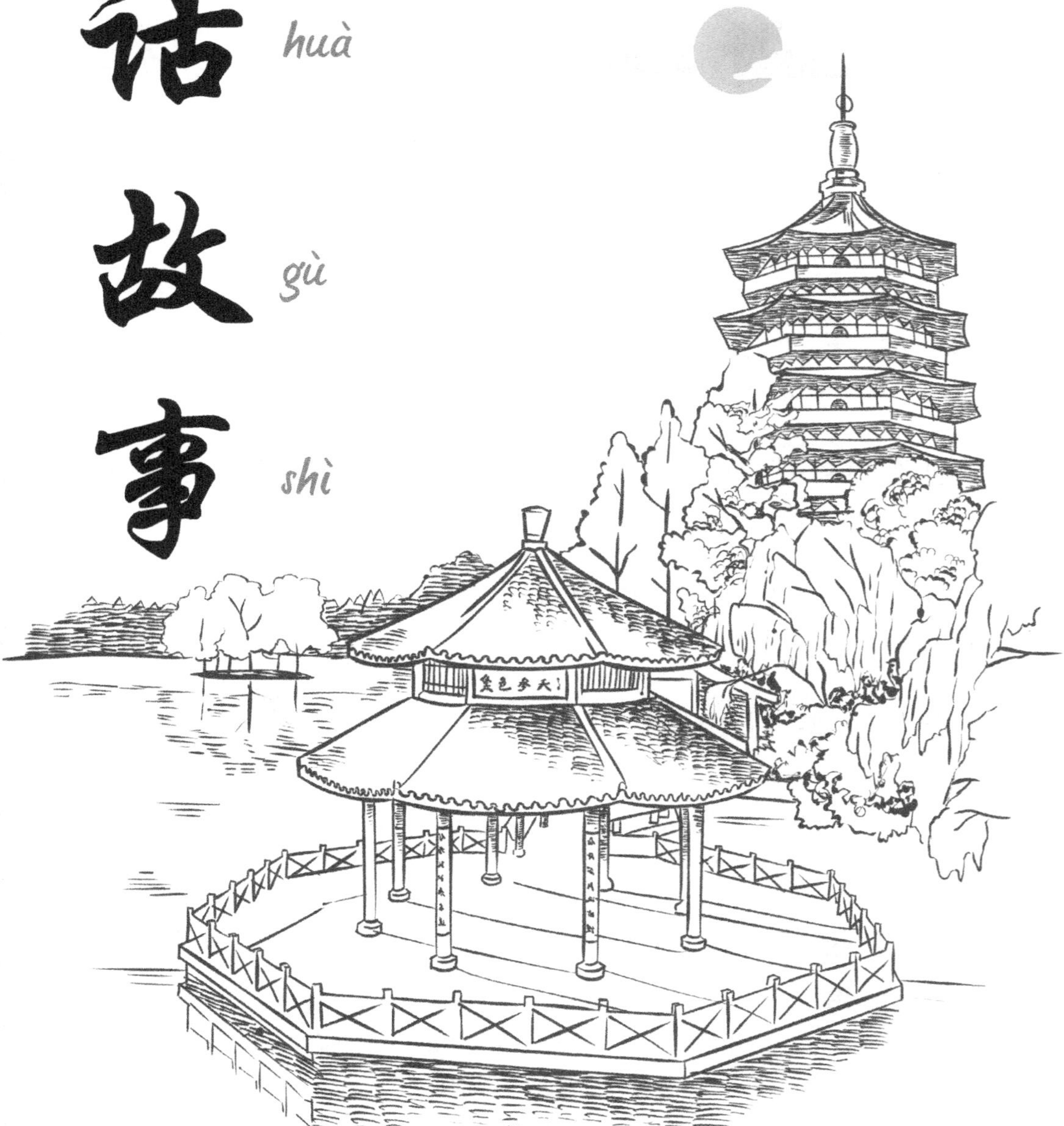

cháng é bēn yuè

嫦娥奔月

Chang'e Flying to the Moon

gǔ shí hòu tiān shàng tū rán chū xiàn le shí gè tài yáng

古时候，**天上**突然出现了十个**太阳**。

In ancient times, **in the sky** ten **suns** suddenly appeared.

dà dì biàn de hěn gān zào rén men de shēng huó hěn kùn nán

大地**变得**很**干燥**，人们的生活很**困难**。

The land **became** very **dry** and people's lives were very **difficult**.

zhí dào yí gè jiào hòu yì de yīng xióng chū xiàn le

直到，一个叫后羿的**英雄**出现了。

Until, a **hero** named Hou Yi appeared.

yì tiān tā pá dào shān dǐng yòng shén qí de gōng jiàn shè xià le jiǔ gè tài yáng

一天，他爬到**山顶**，用神奇的**弓箭**射下了九个太阳。

One day, he climbed to the **top of the mountain** and shot down nine suns with a magical **bow and arrow**.

dà dì dé jiù le tiān dì wèi le gǎn xiè hòu yì jiù sòng gěi le tā yì kē xiān dān

大地得救了，**天帝**为了**感谢**后羿，就送给了他一颗**仙丹**。

The land was saved, and in order **to thank** Hou Yi, the **Heaven emperor** gave him an **elixir**.

shéi chī le tā, jiù néng biàn chéng xiān rén。
谁吃了它，就能变成**仙人**。
Whoever eats it would become an **immortal**.

kě shì, hòu yì shè bu dé lí kāi tā de qī zi cháng é, jiù cáng le xiān dān。
可是，后羿**舍不得**离开他的**妻子**嫦娥，就**藏**了仙丹。
However, Hou Yi was **reluctant** to leave his **wife** Chang'e, so he **hid** the elixir.

zhè jiàn shì chuán kāi hòu, yì tiān wǎn shàng, yí gè xiǎo tōu qù le hòu yì jiā tōu xiān dān。
这件事**传开**后，一天晚上，一个**小偷**去了后羿家**偷**仙丹。
After the story **spread**, one night, a **thief** went to Hou Yi's house to **steal** the elixir.

xiǎo tōu fā xiàn zhǐ yǒu cháng é zài jiā, jiù ná dāo bī cháng é jiāo chū xiān dān。
小偷**发现**只有嫦娥在家，就拿刀**逼**嫦娥**交出**仙丹。
The thief **found** that only Chang'e was at home, so he held a knife **forcing** Chang'e to **hand over** the elixir.

cháng é yòu hài pà yòu zhāo jí, jiù tūn xià le xiān dān。
嫦娥又**害怕**又**着急**，就**吞下**了仙丹。
Chang'e was **afraid** and **anxious**, so she **swallowed** the elixir.

zhè shí hòu yì gāng gāng huí jiā, xiǎo tōu mǎ shàng jiù pǎo le。
这时后羿**刚刚**回家，小偷**马上**就跑了。
At this time, Hou Yi had **just** returned home, and the thief ran away **immediately**.

kě shì, hěn kuài cháng é de shēn tǐ yuè lái yuè qīng, tā fēi le qǐ lái。
可是，很快嫦娥的身体**越来越轻**，她**飞了起来**。
However, soon Chang'e's body became **lighter and lighter**, and she **flew up**.

hòu yì jìn quán lì qù lā cháng é, kě shì lā bu zhù,
后羿**尽全力**去**拉**嫦娥，可是拉不住，
Hou Yi **tried his best** to **pull** Chang'e, but he couldn't.

tā yuè fēi yuè gāo, fēi dào le yuè liàng, biàn chéng le yuè shén。
她越飞越高，飞到了**月亮**，变成了**月神**。
She flew higher and higher, until she reached **the Moon**, becoming the **Moon goddess**.

nà tiān shì bā yuè shí wǔ, yuè liàng yòu dà yòu yuán

那天是八月十五，月亮**又**大**又**圆。

That day was the 15th day of the 8th month, and the Moon was big **and** round.

hòu yì kàn zhe yuè liàng, fēi cháng xiǎng cháng é

后羿看着**月亮**，非常**想**嫦娥，

Hou Yi was looking at **the moon** and **missed** Chang'e very much.

hòu lái, tā měi nián zhè tiān dōu huì zuò yuè bǐng jì niàn cháng é

后来，他**每年**这天**都**会做月饼纪念嫦娥。

Later, **every year** on this day, he **always** made mooncakes to commemorate Chang'e.

bā yuè shí wǔ chéng wéi le zhōng qiū jié, chī yuè bǐng yě chéng wéi le zhōng qiū jié de chuán tǒng

八月十五成为了**中秋节**，吃**月饼**也成为了中秋节的**传统**。

The 15th day of the 8th month (lunar calendar) became the **Mid-Autumn Festival**, and eating **mooncakes** also became a **tradition** of the festival.

I pray our life be long! Though far apart,
the Moon keeps together our soul and heart.

- SU SHI -

Culture Corner

The **Mid-Autumn Festival** (zhōng qiū jié 中秋节), the second biggest in China, falls on the 15th day of the 8th month in lunar calendar, and the story of Chang'e Flying to the Moon is the origin of it. In modern China people enjoy a 3-day public holiday. These days bā yuè 八月 typically refers to "August" but traditional Chinese festivals are celebrated according to the Chinese lunar calendar and fall on a different date in the Gregorian calendar each year.

In Chinese culture, people also have always held special feelings towards the full round moon as it symbolizes **reunion** (tuán yuán 团圆), reminding them of the loved ones far away. Hence the festival is one of reunion. Having reunion meals with family, eating mooncakes, watching the Moon, and lighting up lanterns are all common festive activities. The rabbit is also a symbol of this festival as it is the pet of Chang'e.

People often argue that if Hou Yi didn't hide the elixir, he and Chang'e would not end up with such a sad ending. **Imagine you were Hou Yi, what will you do with the elixir?**

A
zì jǐ chī
自己吃
Eat it myself

B
qǐng tiān dì zài sòng yì kē gěi cháng é
请天帝再送一颗给嫦娥
Ask the heaven emperor to give one to Chang'e

C
rēng le tā
扔了它
Throw it away

D
mài le tā, huò zhě sòng gěi bié rén
卖了它，或者送给别人
Sell it or give it away

KEY VOCABULARY

tài yáng 太阳	*n.*	the Sun	fā xiàn 发现	*v.*	to find/notice
gān zào 干燥	*adj.*	dry	hài pà 害怕	*adj.*	scared
kùn nán 困难	*adj.*	difficult	zhāo jí 着急	*adj.*	anxious
yīng xióng 英雄	*n.*	hero	gāng gāng 刚刚	*adv.*	just (time)
gǎn xiè 感谢	*v.*	to thank	mǎ shàng 马上	*adv.*	immediately
lí kāi 离开	*v.*	to leave	yuè liàng 月亮	*n.*	the Moon
qī zi 妻子	*n.*	wife	yuè bǐng 月饼	*n.*	mooncake
xiǎo tōu 小偷	*n.*	thief	jì niàn 纪念	*v.*	to commemorate
tōu 偷	*v.*	to steal	zhōng qiū jié 中秋节	*n.*	Mid-Autumn Festival

SENTENCE PATTERNS

yuè lái yuè
越来越 ...

more and more ...

yuè lái yuè
越来越 + *adj*

tā de shēn tǐ yuè lái yuè qīng
她的身体越来越轻。

Her body is getting lighter and lighter.

měi dōu
每 ... 都 ...

to emphasize frequency of event

měi dōu
每 + *time* + **都** + *event*

tā měi nián zhè tiān dōu huì zuò yuè bǐng jì niàn cháng é
他每年这天都会做月饼纪念嫦娥。

Every year on this day, he always made mooncakes to commemorate Chang'e.

Chinese version

古时候，天上突然出现了十个太阳。

大地变得很干燥，人们的生活很困难。

直到，一个叫后羿的英雄出现了。

一天，他爬到山顶，用神奇的弓箭射下了九个太阳。

大地得救了，天帝为了感谢后羿，就送给了他一颗仙丹。

谁吃了它，就能变成仙人。

可是，后羿舍不得离开他的妻子嫦娥，就藏了仙丹。

这件事传开后，一天晚上，一个小偷去了后羿家偷仙丹。

小偷发现只有嫦娥在家，就拿刀逼嫦娥交出仙丹。

嫦娥又害怕又着急，就吞下了仙丹。

这时后羿刚刚回家，小偷马上就跑了。

可是，很快嫦娥的身体越来越轻，她飞了起来。

后羿尽全力去拉嫦娥，可是拉不住，

她越飞越高，飞到了月亮，变成了月神。

那天是八月十五，月亮又大又圆。

后羿看着月亮，非常想嫦娥，

后来，他每年这天都会做月饼纪念嫦娥。

八月十五成为了中秋节，吃月饼也成为了中秋节的传统。

měi hóu wáng

美猴王

2 The Monkey King (Origin Story)

cóng qián, yǒu yí zuò huā guǒ shān。 shān shàng yǒu yí kuài shén qí de dà shí tou。

从前，有一座**花果山**。山上有一块**神奇**的大石头。

Once upon a time, there was a **Mount of Flowers and Fruits**, with a **magical** rock on the mountain.

yì tiān, shí tou tū rán liè kāi, tiào chū le yì zhī shí hóu。

一天，石头**突然**裂开，**跳出**了一只石猴。

One day, the rock **suddenly** cracked, and a stone monkey **jumped out**.

tā bù jǐn néng zǒu néng pǎo, ér qiě néng chī néng hē。

它**不仅**能走能跑，**而且**能吃能喝。

He was **not only** able to walk and run, **but also** able to eat and drink.

tiān qì hěn rè, shí hóu hé qí tā hóu zi men qù hé biān xǐ zǎo。

天气很热，石猴和**其他**猴子们去河边**洗澡**。

The **weather** was very hot, and the stone monkey went to the river to **take a bath** with **other** monkeys.

tā men zài xǐ zǎo de shí hòu, tǎo lùn hé shuǐ lái zì nǎ lǐ。

它们**在**洗澡**的时候**，**讨论**河水**来自**哪里。

When they were bathing, they **discussed** where the river water **came from**.

yú shì, dà jiā kāi shǐ shùn zhe shuǐ liú zǒu。

于是，大家**开始**顺着**水流**走。

So, everyone **started** walking along the **stream**.

hěn kuài, tā men kàn jiàn le yí gè dà pù bù. dà jiā dōu xiǎng zhī dào lǐ miàn shì shén me, dàn bù gǎn jìn qù.

很快，它们看见了一个大**瀑布**。大家都想知道**里面**是什么，但**不敢**进去。

Soon, they saw a big **waterfall**. Everyone wanted to know what was **inside**, but **dare not** to go in.

hòu lái, yǒu xiē hóu zi shuō: "shéi gǎn jìn qù kàn kan, jiù shì hóu wáng."

后来，有些猴子说："谁敢**进去**看看，就是**猴王**。"

Later, some monkeys said, "Whoever dares to **go in** to take a look is the **Monkey King**."

mǎ shàng, shí hóu jiù zhàn chū lái, dà shēng shuō: "wǒ gǎn!" rán hòu, tā tiào jìn le pù bù.

马上，石猴就**站出来**，大声说："我**敢**!"然后，它**跳进**了瀑布。

Immediately, the stone monkey **stood up** and said loudly: "I **dare**!" Then he **jumped into** the waterfall.

tā gāo xìng de fā xiàn: lǐ miàn hěn dà, hěn měi, yǒu shí zhuō zǐ、shí yǐ zǐ hé shí chuáng.

它高兴地**发现**：里面很大，很美，有石**桌子**、石**椅子**和石**床**。

He happily **discovered** that it was huge and beautiful inside, and had stone **tables**, stone **chairs**, and stone **beds**.

yú shì, tā pǎo chū qù gào sù hóu zi men, ràng hóu zi men yì qǐ jìn lái.

于是，它跑出去**告诉**猴子们，让猴子们**一起**进来。

So, he ran out to **tell** other monkeys about it, letting them come in **together**.

dà jiā kàn dào hòu, fēi cháng gāo xīng. tā men hěn xǐ huān zhè lǐ, jué dìng zài zhè lǐ zhù.

大家看到后，非常**高兴**。它们很喜欢这里，**决定**在这里**住**。

After seeing this, they were extremely **happy**. They liked it very much and **decided** to **live** here.

shí hóu yě chéng wéi le hóu wáng. kě shì, tā jué de zì jǐ shì hěn tè bié, hěn měi de hóu zi.

石猴也**成为**了猴王。**可是**，它觉得自己是很**特别**，很**美**的猴子。

The stone monkey also **became** the monkey king. **However**, he felt himself a very **special** and **good-looking** monkey.

suǒ yǐ, tā ràng dà jiā jiào tā "měi hóu wáng".

所以，它让大家叫它"美猴王"。

Therefore, he asked everyone to call him "the Good-looking Monkey King".

Culture Corner

The Monkey King, later known as **Sun Wukong** (孙悟空 sūn wù kōng) is a legendary mythical figure from the renowned Chinese novel **Journey to the West** (西游记 xī yóu jì).

The story here is about his origin as a stone monkey and how he became the Monkey King. Through the entire story of Journey to the West, the Monkey King was a powerful and rebellious figure who dared to fight with the authorities of Heaven - making him very popular and influential for Chinese people in ancient and modern China. Hence in Chinese culture he is highly regarded as a symbolic force that dares to challenge the dominion power.

The monkey king was very creative and decided to pick the title for himself. What about you? **If you were him, what title would you pick for yourself?**

Key vocabulary

cóng qián 从前	*n.*	once upon a time	zhàn chū lái 站出来	*vp.*	to stand up/come ahead
tū rán 突然	*adj.* *adv.*	sudden suddenly	fā xiàn 发现	*v.*	to notice/discover
tiào 跳	*v.*	to jump	gào sù 告诉	*v.*	to tell
lái zì 来自	*v.*	come from	yì qǐ 一起	*adv.*	together
tiān qì 天气	*n.*	weather	zhù 住	*v.*	to live
xǐ zǎo 洗澡	*v.*	to shower/ take a bath	kě shì 可是	*conj.*	however/yet
dà jiā 大家	*n.*	everyone	chéng wéi 成为	*v.*	to become
pù bù 瀑布	*n.*	waterfall	tè bié 特别	*adj.*	special
jìn qù 进去	*v.*	to enter	suǒ yǐ 所以	*conj.*	hence, so

Sentence patterns

bù jǐn ér qiě
不仅 … 而且 …

not only … but also …

bù jǐn ér qiě
subject + **不仅** + *feature 1* + **而且** + *feature 2*

tā bù jǐn néng zǒu néng pǎo, ér qiě néng chī néng hē
它不仅能走能跑，而且能吃能喝。

He was not only able to walk and run, but also able to eat and drink.

zài de shí hòu
在 … 的时候 …

when/at the time of …

zài de shí hòu
在 + *verb* + **的时候** + *clause*

tā men zài xǐ zǎo de shí hòu, tǎo lùn hé shuǐ lái zì nǎ lǐ
它们在洗澡的时候，讨论河水来自哪里。

When they were bathing, they discussed where the river water came from.

CHINESE VERSION

从前，有一座花果山。山上有一块神奇的大石头。

一天，石头突然裂开，跳出了一只石猴。

它不仅能走能跑，而且能吃能喝。

天气很热，石猴和其他猴子们去河边洗澡。

它们在洗澡的时候，讨论河水来自哪里。

于是，大家开始顺着水流走。

很快，它们看见了一个大瀑布。大家都想知道里面是什么，但不敢进去。

后来，有些猴子说："谁敢进去看看，就是猴王。"

马上，石猴就站出来，大声说："我敢"！然后，它跳掉进了瀑布。

它高兴地发现：里面很大，很美，有石桌子、石椅子和石床。

于是，它跑出去告诉猴子们，让猴子们一起进来。

大家看到后，非常高兴。它们很喜欢这里，决定在这里住。

石猴也成为了猴王。可是，它觉得自己是很特别，很美的猴子。

所以，它让大家叫它"美猴王"。

bái shé zhuàn

白蛇传

The Legend of the White Snake

yì qiān duō nián qián, liǎng gè hěn měi de nǚ zǐ zài xī hú sàn bù.

一**千**多年前，两个很美的女子在西湖**散步**。

More than **a thousand** years ago, two very beautiful women were **walking** by the West Lake

tā men yí gè jiào bái sù zhēn, lìng yí gè jiào xiǎo qīng.

她们一个叫白素贞，**另一个**叫小青。

One of them was called Bai Suzhen and **the other** Xiaoqing.

tā men bú shì rén, ér shì bái shé yāo hé qīng shé yāo.

她们不是**人**，而是白**蛇妖**和青**蛇妖**。

They were not **humans**, but the white **snake demon** and the green **snake demon**.

kě shì, tā men shì shàn liáng de yāo, cháng cháng bāng zhù rén.

可是，他们是**善良**的妖，常常**帮助**人。

However, they were **kind-hearted** demons, who often **helped** people.

yì tiān, bái sù zhēn zài hú biān de qiáo shàng yù dào le yí gè nián qīng nán zǐ xǔ xiān.

一天，白素贞在**湖边**的桥上**遇到**了一个**年轻**男子许仙。

One day, on the bridge **by the lake** Bai Suzhen **encountered** a **young** man Xu Xian.

xǔ xiān shēn shēn de bèi bái sù zhēn de měi xī yǐn le. hěn kuài, tā men jiù xiāng ài le.

许仙深深地**被**白素贞的美**吸引**了。很快，他们就**相爱**了。

Xu Xian was deeply **attracted by** Bai Suzhen's beauty. Soon, they **fell in love**.

yǒu xiǎo qīng de zhī chí xǔ xiān hé bái sù zhēn jié hūn le
有小青的**支持**，许仙和白素贞**结婚**了。
With Xiaoqing's **support**, Xu Xian and Bai Suzhen **got married**.

xǔ xiān shì gè yī shēng tā zài zhèn shàng kāi le yí gè zhěn suǒ
许仙是个**医生**，他在**镇**上开了一个**诊所**。
Xu Xian was a **doctor**, he opened a **clinic** in the **town**.

bái sù zhēn bāng xǔ xiān guǎn lǐ hái jīng cháng miǎn fèi yī zhì qióng rén
白素贞帮许仙**管理**，还经常**免费**医治穷人。
Bai Suzhen helped Xu Xian with **management** and often treated the poor **free of charge**.

kě shì yǒu yì tiān yí gè lǎo hé shàng lái dào zhěn suǒ dài zǒu le xǔ xiān
可是，有一天，一个老**和尚**来到诊所，**带走**了许仙。
However, one day, an old **monk** came to the clinic and **took away** Xu Xian,

tā shuō bái sù zhēn shì gè shé yāo kě shì xǔ xiān bù xiāng xìn
他说白素贞是个**蛇妖**。可是许仙不**相信**。
He said that Bai Suzhen was a **snake demon**. But Xu Xian didn't **believe** it.

bái sù zhēn hé xiǎo qīng lái dào sì miào jiù xǔ xiān gēn hé shàng dǎ jià
白素贞和小青来到**寺庙**救许仙，**跟**和尚**打架**。
Bai Suzhen and Xiaoqing came to the **temple** to rescue Xu Xian and **fought with** the monk.

bái sù zhēn ràng xiǎo qīng dài zǒu xǔ xiān zì jǐ què bèi hé shàng guān jìn le léi fēng tǎ
白素贞让小青**带走**许仙，**自己**却被和尚关进了**雷峰塔**。
Bai Suzhen asked Xiaoqing to **take** Xu Xian **away**, but she **herself** was imprisoned in **Leifeng Pagoda** by the monk.

shí nián hòu xiǎo qīng biàn de gèng qiáng tā cuī huǐ le léi fēng tǎ jiù le bái sù zhēn
十年后，小青变得**更强**，她**摧毁**了雷锋塔，**救**了白素贞。
Ten years later, Xiaoqing became **stronger**, she **destroyed** Lei Feng Pagoda and **rescued** Bai Suzhen.

zuì hòu xǔ xiān yě jiē shòu le bái sù zhēn tā yì zhí dōu ài zhe tā
最后，许仙也**接受**了白素贞，他**一直**都爱着她。
In the end, Xu Xian also **accepted** Bai Suzhen, he had **always** loved her.

tā zài yě bú zài hu tā shì shé yāo zhǐ xiǎng yǒng yuǎn hé tā zài yì qǐ
他再也不**在乎**她是蛇妖，只想**永远**和她**在一起**。
He didn't **care** she was a snake demon any more, and just wanted **to be with** her **forever**.

Culture Corner

The Legend of the White Snake (白蛇传 bái shé zhuàn) is widely known and considered one of China's four great folktales, appearing in numerous stage shows, operas, and films. Even today many people still go to the West Lake (in Hangzhou city, China) to visit the Leifeng Pagoda, which has become one of the hottest scenic spots of the city.

In the full story, after Xu Xian knew Bai Suzheng was a snake demon, he was scared and struggled with it for a very long time before he overcame it and decided to accept Bai Suzheng.

If this happened to you, what would you do?

A
lí kāi bái sù zhēn
离开白素贞
Leave Bai Suzheng

B
jiē shòu bái sù zhēn
接受白素贞
Accept Bai Suzheng

C
bù zuò fū qī, zhī zuò péng yǒu
不做夫妻，只做朋友
End the marriage, just be friends

D
bù zhī dào
不知道
Don't know/not sure

Key vocabulary

sàn bù 散步	*v.*	to walk
shàn liáng 善良	*adj.*	kind-hearted
bāng zhù 帮(助)	*v.*	to help
xī yǐn 吸引	*v.*	to attract
xiāng ài 相爱	*v.*	to fall in love
zhī chí 支持	*v.* *n.*	to support support
jié hūn 结婚	*n.*	to get married
yī shēng 医生	*n.*	doctor
zhěn suǒ 诊所	*n.*	clinic
guǎn lǐ 管理	*v.* *n.*	to manage management
miǎn fèi 免费	*adj.*	free (of charge)
xiāng xìn 相信	*adj.*	to believe
cuī huǐ 摧毁	*v.*	to destroy
dǎ jià 打架	*v.*	to fight (physically)
jiē shòu 接受	*v.*	to accept
yì zhí 一直	*adv.*	always
zài hu 在乎	*v.*	to care/mind
yǒng yuǎn 永远	*adj.*	forever

Sentence patterns

bèi xī yǐn ... 被 ... 吸引

... attracted by ...

A + bèi 被 + *B* + xī yǐn 吸引

xǔ xiān shēn shēn de bèi bái sù zhēn de měi xī yǐn le
许仙深深地被白素贞的美吸引了。

Xu Xian was deeply attracted by Bai Suzhen's beauty.

gēn dǎ jià 跟 ... 打架

fight with ...

A + gēn 跟 + *B* + dǎ jià 打架

tā men gēn hé shàng dǎ jià
她们跟和尚打架。

They fought with the monk.

CHINESE VERSION

一千多年前，两个很美的女子在西湖散步。

她们一个叫白素贞，另一个叫小青。

她们不是人，而是白蛇妖和青蛇妖。

可是，他们是善良的妖，常常帮助人。

一天，白素贞在湖边的桥上遇到了一个年轻男子许仙。

许仙深深地被白素贞的美吸引了。很快，他们就相爱了。

有小青的支持，许仙和白素贞结婚了。

许仙是个医生，他在镇上开了一个诊所。

白素贞帮许仙管理，还经常免费医治穷人。

可是，有一天，一个老和尚来到诊所，带走了许仙。

他说白素贞是个蛇妖。可是许仙不相信。

白素贞和小青来到寺庙救许仙，跟和尚打架。

白素贞让小青带走许仙，自己却被和尚关进了雷峰塔。

十年后，小青变得更强，她摧毁了雷锋塔，救了白素贞。

最后，许仙也接受了白素贞，他一直都爱着她。

他再也不在乎她是蛇妖，只想永远和她在一起。

niú láng zhī nǚ

牛郎织女

The Cowherd and Weaver Girl

hěn jiǔ yǐ qián, tiān shàng zhù zhe yí wèi hěn měi de gōng zhǔ, jiào zhī nǚ.

很久以前，**天上**住着一位很美的**公主**，叫织女。

A long time ago, there was a beautiful **princess** living in **heaven** named Weaver Girl.

tā shàn cháng zhī bù, hái zhī le zuì měi de cǎi hóng.

她**擅长**织布，还织了最美的**彩虹**。

She was **good at** weaving cloth, and also weaved the most beautiful **rainbow**.

kě shì, tā jué de zhè zhǒng shēng huó hěn wú liáo, jiù qiāo qiāo qù le rén jiān.

可是，她觉得**这种**生活很**无聊**，就**悄悄**去了人间。

However, she felt **this type of** life is very **boring**, so she went to the mortal world **in secret**.

zhī nǚ zài rén jiān lǚ yóu, rèn shi le jiào niú láng de nián qīng nán zǐ.

织女在人间**旅游**，认识了叫牛郎的**年轻男子**。

The Weaver Girl **travelled** in the mortal world and met a **young man** named Cowherd.

niú láng suī rán shì gè fàng niú de nóng mín, dàn shì hěn shuài, hěn shàn liáng.

牛郎**虽然**是个放牛的农民，**但是**很帅、很善良。

Although Cowherd was just a farmer who attended cattle, (**but**) he was very handsome and kind.

màn màn de, zhī nǚ hé niú láng xiāng ài le.

慢慢地，织女和牛郎**相爱**了。

Gradually, the Weaver Girl and Cowherd **fell in love**.

tā men qiāo qiāo jié hūn le hái yǒu le liǎng gè kě ài de hái zi
他们悄悄**结婚**了，还有了两个**可爱**的孩子。

They **got married** secretly and had two **lovely** children.

kě shì yǒu yì tiān zhī nǚ de wài pó zhǎo dào le tā men
可是，有一天，织女的**外婆**找到了他们。

However, one day, the Weaver Girl's **grandmother** found them.

wài pó hěn shēng qì tā jué de fán rén bú pèi hé xiān rén zài yì qǐ
jiù zhuā zǒu le zhī nǚ
外婆很**生气**，她觉得凡人**不配**和仙人在一起，就**抓走**了织女。

The grandmother was very **angry**, she felt that mortals were **not worthy** to be with the immortals, so she **arrested** the Weaver Girl.

huí dào tiān shàng hòu zhī nǚ shāng xīn jí le bú zài zhī bù
回到天上后，织女**伤心**极了，**不再**织布。

After **returning to** heaven, the Weaver Girl was so **sad** that she **stopped** weaving.

wèi le ràng zhī nǚ jì xù zhī bù wài pó tóng yì tā zài měi nián qī yuè
qī rì hé niú láng jiàn miàn
为了让织女**继续**织布，外婆**同意**她在每年七月七日**和**牛郎**见面**。

In order to make the Weaver Girl **continue** weaving, the grandmother **agreed** for her **to meet with** the Cowherd on 7th day of the 7th month once a year.

nà tiān xǐ què men huì zài tiān shàng wèi tā men dā qiáo
那天，**喜鹊**们会在天上为他们**搭桥**。

On that day, the **magpies** would **tower the bridge** for them in the sky.

hòu lái zhè yì tiān jiù chéng wéi le zhōng guó de qíng rén jié yě jiào qī
xī jié
后来，**这一天**就成为了中国的**情人节**，也叫**七夕节**。

Later, **this day** became China's **Valentine's Day**, which is also called **Qixi Festival**.

Culture Corner

The **Qi Xi Festival** (七夕节 qī xī jié), also known as Double Seventh Festival, falls on the 7th day of the 7th month in lunar calendar. It is the Chinese Valentine's Day and the story of **the cowherd and weaver girl** (牛郎织女 niú láng zhī nǚ) is the origin of it. The **Star of Altair** (牵牛星 qiān niú xīng) and the **Star of Vega** (织女星 zhī nǚ xīng) are also named after them in Chinese. In China, people often propose or get married on this day.

For the cowherd and weaver girl, it is very harsh to only meet one another one day a year. **Imagine that you could also only meet your beloved one day a year, will you still carry on with the relationship?**

A
kě néng huì
可能会
Possibly will

B
yí dìng huì
一定会
Definitely will

C
dāng rán bù huì
当然不会
Of course not

D
děi kàn qíng kuàng
得看情况
Depends on the situation

Key vocabulary

hěn jiǔ 很久	*n.*	a long time	kě ài 可爱	*adj.*	cute/lovely
gōng zhǔ 公主	*n.*	princess	wài pó 外婆	*n.*	maternal grandmother
shàn cháng 擅长	*v.*	be good at	shēng qì 生气	*adj.*	angry
cǎi hóng 彩虹	*n.*	rainbow	huí dào 回（到）	*v.*	to return to
wú liáo 无聊	*adj.*	boring	shāng xīn 伤心	*adj.*	sad/heartbroken
qiāo qiāo 悄悄	*adv.*	in secret/quietly	jì xù 继续	*v.*	to carry on
lǚ yóu 旅游	*v.*	to travel	tóng yì 同意	*v.*	to agree
nóng mín 农民	*n.*	farmer	qíng rén jié 情人节	*n.*	Valentine's Day
shuài 帅	*adj.*	handsome	qī xī jié 七夕节	*n.*	Qi Xi Festival

Sentence patterns

suī rán dàn shì
虽然 … 但是 …

although … (but) …

suī rán 虽然 + *sentence* + dàn shì 但是 + *contradictory sentence*

niú láng suī rán shì gè fàng niú de nóng mín, dàn shì hěn shuài、hěn shàn liáng.
牛郎虽然是个放牛的农民，但是很帅、很善良。

Although Cowherd was just a farmer who attended cattle, (but) he was very handsome and kind.

hé jiàn miàn
和 … 见面 …

to meet (up with)…

A + hé 和 + *B* + jiàn miàn 见面

tā zài měi nián qī yuè qī rì hé niú láng jiàn miàn.
她在每年七月七日和牛郎见面。

She meets with the Cowherd on 7th day of the 7th month every year.

CHINESE VERSION

很久以前，天上住着一位很美的公主，叫织女。

她擅长织布，还织了最美的彩虹。

可是，她觉得这种生活很无聊，就悄悄去了人间。

织女在人间旅游，认识了叫牛郎的年轻男子。

牛郎虽然是个放牛的农民，但是很帅、很善良。

慢慢地，织女和牛郎相爱了。

他们悄悄结婚了，还有了两个可爱的孩子。

可是，有一天，织女的外婆找到了他们。

外婆很生气，她觉得凡人不配和仙人在一起，就抓走了织女。

回到天上后，织女伤心极了，不再织布。

为了让织女继续织布，外婆同意她在每年七月七日和牛郎见面。

那天，喜鹊们会在天上为他们塔桥。

后来，这一天就成为了中国的情人节，也叫七夕节。

寓言故事

yù yán gù shì

Chinese Fables

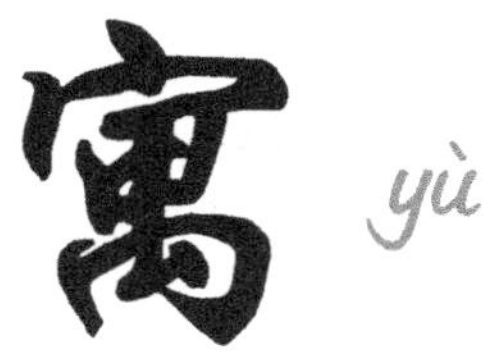

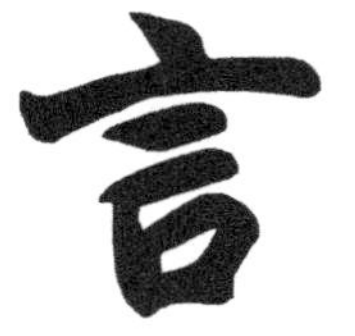

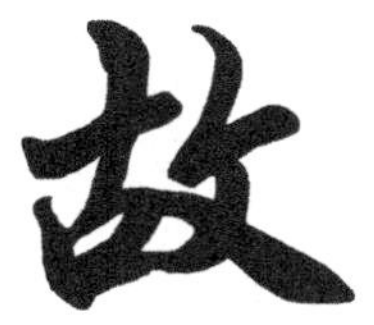

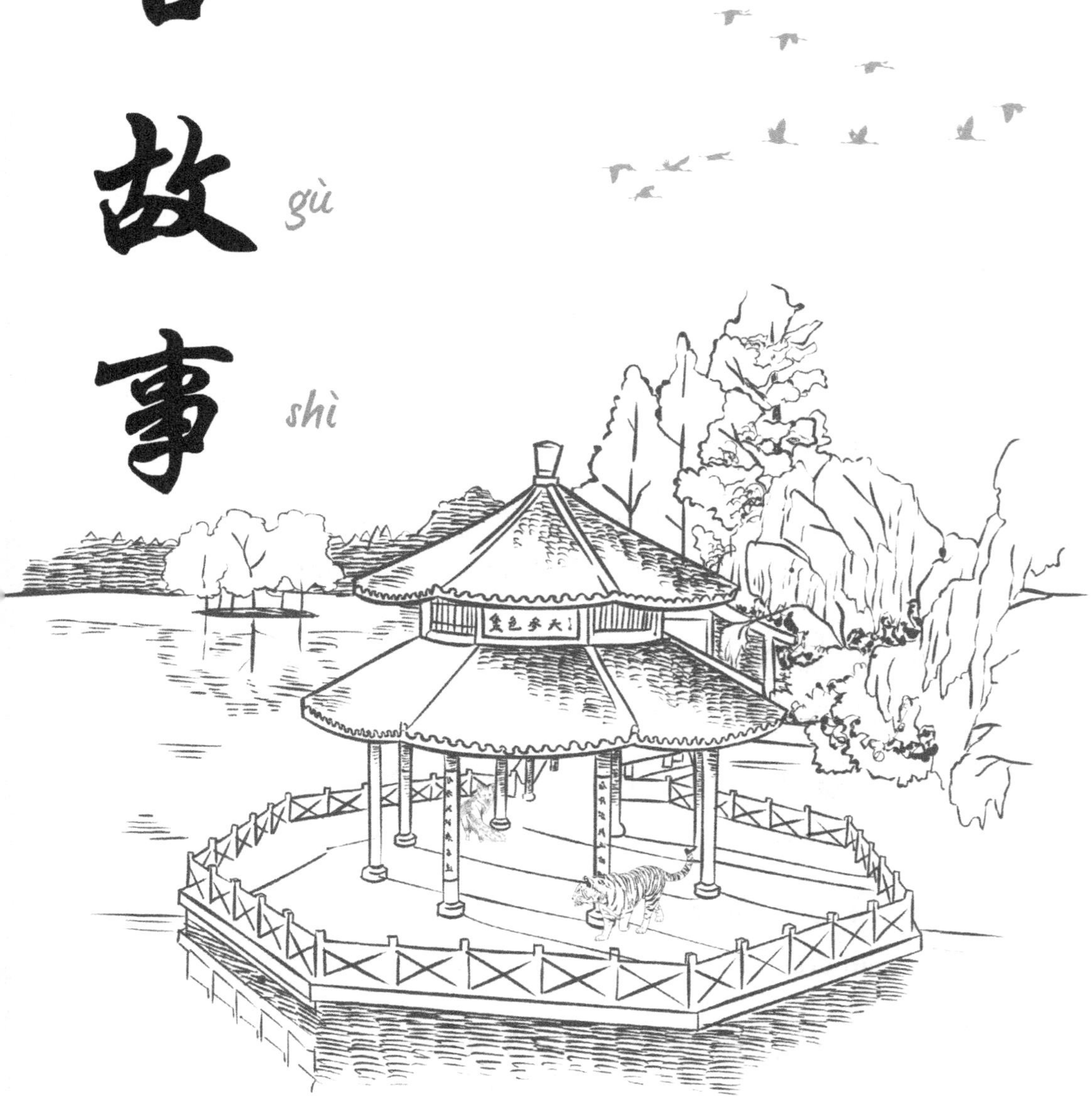

shǒu zhū dài tù

5 守株待兔

Waiting for Hares Under a Tree

sòng guó yǒu gè nóng mín, tā měi tiān zài tián lǐ nǔ lì gàn huó。
宋国有个**农民**，他**每天**在田里**努力**干活。
In the state of Song, there was a **farmer** who **worked hard** in the fields **everyday**.

zhè kuài tián hěn dà, shàng miàn yǒu yì kē dà shù。
这块**田**很大，上面有一棵**大树**。
The **field** is very big and there is a **big tree** on it.

yì tiān, tā zài gàn huó de shí hòu, hū rán kàn jiàn yì zhī bēn pǎo de tù zi。
一天，他在**干活**的时候，**忽然**看见一只**奔跑**的兔子。
One day, while he was **working**, he **suddenly** saw a **running** rabbit.

tù zi yuè pǎo yuè kuài, xiàng jiàn yí yàng chōng guò lái。
兔子**越跑越快**，像**箭**一样冲过来。
The rabbit **ran faster and faster**, rushing over like an **arrow**.

rán hòu, tā zhuàng zài dà shù shàng, duàn le bó zi, lì kè sǐ le。
然后，它**撞**在大树上，断了**脖子**，**立刻**死了。
Then it **hit** a big tree, broke its **neck**, and died **instantly**.

nóng mín pǎo guò qù, jiǎn qǐ le tù zi, fēi cháng gāo xìng。
农民**跑过去**，**捡起**了兔子，非常高兴。
The farmer **ran over**, **picked up** the rabbit, and was very happy.

tā shuō: "wǒ jīn tiān zhēn xìng yùn, bú yòng gàn huó jiù jiǎn le gè dà pián yi。"
他说："我今天真**幸运**，不用**干活**就捡了个**大便宜**。"
He said: "I'm so **lucky** today, I got a **good deal** without having to **work**."

tā tí zhe tù zi huí jiā, yì biān chàng gē, yì biān tiào wǔ.
他提着兔子回家，**一边**唱歌，**一边**跳舞。
He carried the rabbit home, singing **while** dancing.

tā xiǎng: míng tiān yí dìng hái yǒu tù zi lái, wǒ bù néng cuò guò.
他想：明天**一定**还有兔子来，我不能**错过**。
He thought: Tomorrow, rabbits will **definitely** come again, I can't **miss** it.

dì èr tiān, tā dào tián lǐ, bú zài gàn huó, jiù zuò zài nà kē dà shù xià děng tù zi.
第二天，他到田里，**不再**干活，**就**坐在那棵大树下**等**兔子。
The next day, he went to the field and **stopped** working, **just** sat down under the big tree **waiting for** the rabbit.

kě shì, tā děng le yì tiān, yě méi yǒu tù zi.
可是，他等了**一天**，也没有兔子。
However, after waiting for **a day**, there was no rabbit.

tā bú fàng qì, hòu lái, měi tiān zuò zài nà kē dà shù xià děng tù zi.
他不**放弃**，后来，**每天**坐在那棵大树下等兔子。
He didn't **give up**. Later, he sat under the big tree **every day** waiting for the rabbit.

zhǐ shì, yí gè xīng qī guò qù le, méi yǒu tù zi; yí gè yuè guò qù le, hái shì méi yǒu tù zi.
只是，一个星期**过去了**，没有兔子；一个月**过去了**，**还是**没有兔子。
However, a week **passed**, and there were no rabbits; a month **passed**, and there were **still** no rabbits.

bàn nián le, tián lǐ de cǎo hé tā yí yàng gāo le, kě shì tù zi hái shì méi lái.
半年了，田里的草**和**他**一样**高了，可是兔子**还是**没来。
Half a year passed, and the grass in the field was **as** tall **as** him, but rabbits were **still** not coming.

zhè shí hòu tā cái fā xiàn zì jǐ yì zhí zài kōng děng.
这时候他才**发现**自己**一直**在空等。
Only then did he **realize** that he himself had **always** been waiting in vain.

bié rén dōu zài qìng zhù tián lǐ de fēng shōu, zhǐ yǒu tā, shén me yě méi yǒu.
别人都在**庆祝**田里的**丰收**，**只有**他，什么也没有。
Others were **celebrating** the **harvest** in the fields, **only** for him there was nothing.

SUMMARY

The fable tells us that we cannot rely on luck and those who want to succeed without working are unrealistic. Success and achievement come from **commitment** (坚持 jiān chí) and **hard-working** (努力 nǔ lì), not **luck** (运气 yùn qì) or **laziness** (懒惰 lǎn duò).

Learning Tip

守株待兔 (shǒu zhū dài tù) is a Chinese fable and idiom, translated as: Waiting for Hares Under a Tree. It is used to describe wanting to achieve something but doing nothing towards it.

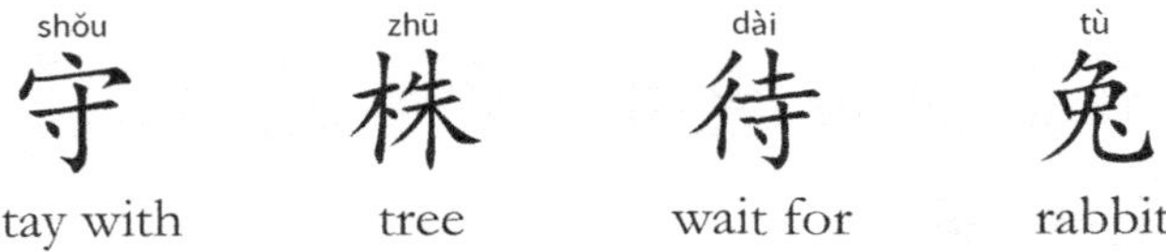

1 我们要创造机会，不能**守株待兔**。
(wǒ men yào chuàng zào jī huì, bù néng shǒu zhū dài tù.)
We have to create opportunities, cannot **just wait and do nothing**.

2 他想要很多钱，但是不工作，天天**守株待兔**。
(tā xiǎng yào hěn duō qián, dàn shì bù gōng zuò, tiān tiān shǒu zhū dài tù.)
He wants a lot of money, but he doesn't work, **just waits and do nothing** every day.

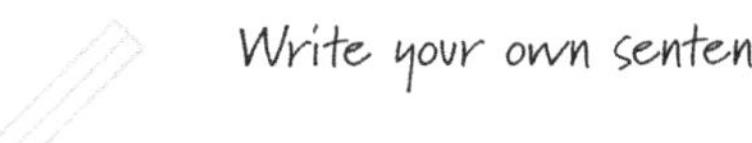

Key vocabulary

hū rán 忽然	*adv.*	suddenly	yí dìng 一定	*adv.*	definitely
měi tiān 每天	*n.*	everyday	cuò guò 错过	*v.*	to miss (out)
gàn huó 干活	*v.*	to work (heavy labor)	děng 等	*v.*	to wait (for)
bēn pǎo 奔跑	*v.*	to run	fàng qì 放弃	*v.*	to give up
lì kè 立刻	*adv.*	immediately	bàn nián 半年	*n.*	half a year
xìng yùn 幸运	*adj.*	lucky	fā xiàn 发现	*v.*	to realize/ notice
dà pián yi 大便宜	*slang*	a good deal (big cheap)	yì zhí 一直	*adv.*	always
chàng gē 唱歌	*v.*	to sing	qìng zhù 庆祝	*v.*	to celebrate
tiào wǔ 跳舞	*v.*	to dance	zhǐ yǒu 只有	*conj.*	only

Sentence patterns

yuè 越 ... yuè 越 ...

the more... the more...

yuè 越 + *verb* + yuè 越 + *adj*

tù zi yuè pǎo yuè kuài
兔子越跑越快。

The rabbit ran faster and faster.

yì biān 一边 ... yì biān 一边 ...

indicates simultaneous actions

yì biān 一边 + *action 1* + yì biān 一边 + *action 2*

tā yì biān chàng gē, yì biān tiào wǔ
他一边唱歌，一边跳舞。

He was singing while dancing.

CHINESE VERSION

宋国有个农民，他每天在田里努力干活。

这块田很大，上面有一棵大树。

一天，他在干活的时候，忽然看见一只奔跑的兔子。

兔子越跑越快，像箭一样冲过来。

然后，它撞在大树上，断了脖子，立刻死了。

农民跑过去，捡起了兔子，非常高兴。

他说：“我今天真幸运，不用干活就捡了个大便宜。”

他提着兔子回家，一边唱歌，一边跳舞。

他想：明天一定还有兔子来，我不能错过。

第二天，他到田里，不再干活，就坐在那棵大树下等兔子。

可是，他等了一天，也没有兔子。

他不放弃，后来，每天坐在那棵大树下等兔子。

只是，一个星期过去了，没有兔子；一个月过去了，还是没有兔子。

半年了，田里的草和他一样高了，可是兔子还是没来。

这时候他才发现自己一直在空等。

别人都在庆祝田里的丰收，只有他，什么也没有。

bèn niǎo xiān fēi

笨鸟先飞

The Early Bird Catches the Worm

6

yǒu yì zhī niǎo mā ma shēng le liù zhī niǎo bǎo bao, dì liù zhī yòu shòu yòu xiǎo

有一只鸟妈妈**生了**六只鸟宝宝，第六只**又**瘦**又**小。

There was a mother bird who **gave birth to** six baby birds, and the sixth was thin **and** small.

gē ge jiě jie men zǒng shì qī fù tā, jiào tā "xiǎo bèn niǎo"

哥哥姐姐们总是**欺负**它，叫它"小**笨**鸟"。

Brothers and sisters always **bully** it and call it a " little **stupid** bird".

měi cì niǎo mā ma gěi tā men wèi chóng zi, xiǎo bèn niǎo dōu chī de zuì shǎo

每次鸟妈妈给它们**喂**虫子，小笨鸟都吃得**最少**。

Every time the mother bird **fed** them worms, the little stupid bird always ate **the least**.

yīn wèi tā hěn ruò, zuǐ lǐ de chóng zi cháng cháng bèi gē ge jiě jie men qiǎng zǒu

因为它很**弱**，嘴里的虫子**常常**被哥哥姐姐们**抢走**。

Because it was too **weak**, the worms in its mouth were **often snatched away** by brothers and sisters.

yú shì, xiǎo bèn niǎo jué dìng duàn liàn, ràng zì jǐ biàn qiáng

于是，小笨鸟**决定**锻炼，让自己变**强**。

So, the little stupid bird **decided to** exercise to make itself **strong**.

tā měi tiān zǎo shàng hěn zǎo qǐ chuáng, nǔ lì duàn liàn shēn tǐ

它每天早上很早**起床**，**努力**锻炼身体。

It **got up** early every morning and **worked hard** to exercise its body.

hěn kuài tā kě yǐ fēi le rán hòu zì jǐ qù zhǎo chóng zi chī
很快，它可以**飞**了，然后自己去**找**虫子吃。

Soon, it was able to **fly**, then went to **find** worms to eat itself.

zài zǎo shàng gē ge jiě jie men hái méi yǒu qǐ chuáng xiǎo bèn niǎo jiù yǐ jīng chū qù chī chóng zi le
在早上，哥哥姐姐们**还没有**起床，小笨鸟就**已经**出去吃虫子了。

In the mornings, brothers and sisters **had not yet** got up, the little stupid bird had **already** gone out to eat the worms.

dà jiā dōu hěn jīng yà zài yě bù gǎn qī fù tā le
大家都很**惊讶**，再也**不敢**欺负它了。

Everyone was so **surprised** and **dared not** to bully it any more.

dōng tiān dào le xiǎo niǎo men dōu yào fēi qù nán fāng
冬天到了，小鸟们**都**要飞去**南方**。

Winter arrived, and the birds were **all** flying to the **south**.

xiǎo bèn niǎo yě shì dì yī gè dào dá de
小笨鸟也**是**第一个到达**的**。

The little stupid bird **was** also the first to arrive.

dà jiā yě zhōng yú míng bái le xiǎo bèn niǎo zhēn de bú bèn
大家也**终于**明白了：小笨鸟**真**的不笨！

Everyone also **finally** understood: the little stupid bird was **really** not stupid!

SUMMARY

This story tells us that even if we have a disadvantage or are weak in some areas, as long as we are determined to change and are willing to work hard, we can still **surpass others** (超过别人 chāo guò bié rén).

Learning Tip

笨鸟先飞 (bèn niǎo xiān fēi) is a Chinese fable and idiom, translated as "The Early Bird Catches the Worm." It is used to describe being able to surpass others through hard-work, despite having disadvantages.

bèn	niǎo	xiān	fēi
笨	鸟	先	飞
stupid	bird	first	fly

1 wǒ xiǎng kǎo shì chéng gōng, jiù děi bèn niǎo xiān fēi.
我想考试成功，就得**笨鸟先飞**。
I want to succeed in the exam, so I need to **work hard earlier**.

2 tā suī rán zuì ruò, dàn tā bèn niǎo xiān fēi, dì yī gè pá shàng le shān dǐng.
他虽然最弱，但他**笨鸟先飞**，第一个爬上了山顶。
Although he is the weakest, he **set off earlier** and was the first to climb to the top of the mountain.

Write your own sentence

Key vocabulary

shēng 生	*v.*	to give birth to	nǔ lì 努力	*v.*	to work hard
shòu 瘦	*adj.*	slim/thin	duàn liàn 锻炼	*v.*	to exercise
bèn 笨	*adj.*	stupid	yǐ jīng 已经	*adv.*	already
qī fù 欺负	*v.*	to bully	jīng yà 惊讶	*adj.*	surprised/ shocked
měi cì 每次	*n.*	every time	bù gǎn 不敢	*v.*	dare not
ruò 弱	*adj.*	weak	dōng tiān 冬天	*v.*	winter
qiáng 强	*adj.*	strong	nán fāng 南方	*n.*	south
jué dìng 决定	*v.*	to decide	dào dá 到达	*v.*	to arrive
qǐ chuáng 起床	*v.*	to get up	zhōng yú 终于	*adv.*	finally

Sentence patterns

yòu yòu 又 ... 又 ...	**... and ...** yòu yòu **又** + *adj* + **又** + *adj* tā yòu shòu yòu xiǎo 它又瘦又小 *It was thin and small*
shì de 是 ... 的	**to emphasize how or when an event happened** shì de **是** + *thing (to be emphasized)* + **的** xiǎo bèn niǎo yě shì dì yī gè dào dá de 小笨鸟也是第一个到达的。 *The little stupid bird was also the first to arrive.*

CHINESE VERSION

有一只鸟妈妈生了六只鸟宝宝，第六只又瘦又小。

哥哥姐姐们总是欺负它，叫它“小笨鸟”。

每次鸟妈妈给它们喂虫子，小笨鸟都吃得最少。

因为它很弱，嘴里的虫子常常被哥哥姐姐们抢走。

于是，小笨鸟决定锻炼，让自己变强。

它每天早上很早起床，努力锻炼身体。

很快，它可以飞了，然后自己去找虫子吃。

在早上，哥哥姐姐们还没有起床，小笨鸟就已经出去吃虫子了。

大家都很惊讶，再也不敢欺负它了。

冬天到了，小鸟们都要飞去南方。

小笨鸟也是第一个到达的。

大家也终于明白了：小笨鸟真的不笨！

7

hú jiǎ hǔ wēi

狐假虎威

Adorn Oneself with Borrowed Plumes

yì tiān, yì zhī lǎo hǔ zài shù lín lǐ tū rán fā xiàn le yì zhī hú li。

一天，一只**老虎**在**树林**里突然发现了一只**狐狸**。

One day, a **tiger** suddenly found a **fox** in the **woods**.

lǎo hǔ mǎ shàng zhuā zhù le hú li，zhǔn bèi dà chī yí dùn。

老虎马上**抓住**了狐狸，准备**大吃一顿**。

The tiger immediately **caught** the fox and prepared to **have a feast**.

kě shì hú li hěn jiǎo huá, piàn lǎo hǔ shuō：

可是狐狸很**狡猾**，**骗**老虎说：

But the fox was very **cunning** and **lied to** the tiger by saying:

"wǒ shì shàng dì pài lái de bǎi shòu zhī wáng, nǐ rú guǒ chī le wǒ, shàng dì huì chéng fá nǐ。"

"我是**上帝**派来的**百兽之王**，你如果吃了我，上帝会**惩罚**你。"

"I was sent here by **God** to be the **king of beasts**. If you eat me, God will **punish** you."

lǎo hǔ jué de hěn qí guài，jiù wèn："nǐ shì bǎi shòu zhī wáng？yǒu zhèng jù ma？"

老虎觉得很**奇怪**，就问："你是**百兽之王**？有**证据**吗？"

The tiger felt **strange** and asked: "You are the **king of beasts**? Do you have any **proof**?"

hú li huí dá nǐ rú guǒ bù xiāng xìn kě yǐ gēn wǒ zǒu yi zǒu
狐狸**回答**："你如果不**相信**，可以跟我**走一走**，
nǐ huì kàn dào dòng wù men fēi cháng pà wǒ
你会看到**动物们**非常**怕**我。"

The fox **replied**, "If you don't **believe** me, you can **have a walk** with me, and you will see how **scared** the **animals** are of me."

yú shì lǎo hǔ jiù dài zhe hú li qù le sēn lín
于是，老虎就带着狐狸去了**森林**。

So the tiger took the fox to the **forest**.

lǎo hǔ zǒu zài qián miàn hú li zǒu zài hòu miàn
老虎走在**前面**，狐狸走在**后面**。

The tiger walked in **front**, and the fox walked **behind**.

tā men měi dào yí gè dì fāng bù guǎn shì tù zi yáng lù hé xióng
它们每到一个**地方**，**不管**是兔子、羊、鹿和熊，
dōu fēi cháng hài pà
都非常害怕。

Every **place** they went, **whether** it was rabbits, goats, deers or bears, they were **all** so scared.

dà jiā zǒng shì yí kàn dào tā men jiù pǎo le
大家总是**一**看到它们，**就**跑了。

As soon as everyone saw them, they always ran away.

rán hòu hú li jiù duì lǎo hǔ shuō xiàn zài nǐ xiāng xìn le ba wǒ
然后，狐狸就对老虎说："现在你**相信**了吧？我
shì bǎi shòu zhī wáng dà jiā dāng rán pà wǒ
是**百兽之王**，大家**当然**怕我！"

Then the fox said to the tiger: "Now do you **believe** it? I am the **king of beasts, of course** everyone is scared of me!"

lǎo hǔ bù zhī dào dòng wù men pà de qí shí shì tā zì jǐ
老虎不知道**动物们**怕的**其实**是它自己。

The tiger didn't know that the **animals** were **actually** scared of he himself.

tā xuǎn zé le xiāng xìn hú li de huà jiù bǎ tā fàng le
它**选择**了相信狐狸的话，就把它**放**了。

So he **chose to** believe the fox's words and **released** it.

SUMMARY

This story tells us that we need to be **smart** (聪明 cōng míng) to identify those who are simply borrowing the power of someone else to bully. They are not really powerful themselves, so there is no need to be afraid of them.

Learning Tip

狐假虎威 (hú jiǎ hǔ wēi), a Chinese fable and idiom, translated as: Adorn Oneself with Borrowed Plumes. It is used to describe those who bully others by flaunting his or her powerful connections.

1 bàn gōng shì yǒu gè rén hú jiǎ hǔ wēi, dàn shì wǒ men bú pà tā.
办公室有个人**狐假虎威**，但是我们不怕他。
There is a person in the office who **adorns himself with borrowed plumes**, but we are not afraid of him.

2 tā gē ge zài, tā cái gǎn dǎ rén, zhēn shì hú jiǎ hǔ wēi.
他哥哥在，他才敢打人，真是**狐假虎威**。
Only when his older brother is around, he dares to beat people, he is really **adorning himself with borrowed plumes**!

Write your own sentence

Key vocabulary

lǎo hǔ 老虎	*n.*	tiger	qí guài 奇怪	*adj.*	strange
hú li 狐狸	*n.*	fox	zhèng jù 证据	*n.*	proof
shù lín 树林	*n.*	woods	xiāng xìn 相信	*v.*	to believe
sēn lín 森林	*n.*	forest	dòng wù 动物	*n.*	animal
dà chī yí dùn 大吃一顿	*vp.*	have a feast	qián miàn 前面	*n.*	front
jiǎo huá 狡猾	*adj.*	cunning	hòu miàn 后面	*n.*	back
piàn 骗	*v.*	to lie	hài pà (害)怕	*v.*	afraid
bǎi shòu zhī wáng 百兽之王	*idiom*	the king of beasts	dāng rán 当然	*adv.*	of course
chéng fá 惩罚	*v.*	to punish	qí shí 其实	*adv.*	actually

Sentence patterns

bù guǎn dōu
不管…都…

no matter/regardless of … (all) ….

bù guǎn dōu
不管 + *situation* + **都** + *result*

bù guǎn shì tù zi yáng lù hé xióng dōu fēi cháng hài pà
不管是兔子、羊、鹿和熊，都非常害怕。

Whether it was rabbits, goats, deers or bears, they were all so scared.

yī jiù
一…就…

as soon as

yī jiù
subject + **一** + *action 1* + **就** + *action 2*

dà jiā yí kàn dào tā men jiù pǎo le
大家一看到它们，就跑了。

As soon as everyone saw them, they ran away.

Chinese version

一天，一只老虎在树林里突然发现了一只狐狸。

老虎马上抓住了狐狸，准备大吃一顿。

可是狐狸很狡猾，骗老虎说：

“我是上帝派来的百兽之王，你如果吃了我，上帝会惩罚你。”

老虎觉得很奇怪，就问：“你是百兽之王？有证据吗？”

狐狸回答：“你如果不相信，可以跟我走一走，你会看到动物们非常怕我。”

于是，老虎就带着狐狸去了森林。

老虎走在前面，狐狸走在后面。

它们每到一个地方，不管是兔子、羊、鹿和熊，都非常害怕。

大家总是一看到它们，就跑了。

然后，狐狸就对老虎说：“现在你相信了吧？ 我是百兽之王，大家当然怕我！”

老虎不知道动物们怕的其实是它自己。

他选择了相信狐狸的话，就把它放了。

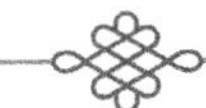

现代故事

xiàn dài gù shì

Modern Stories

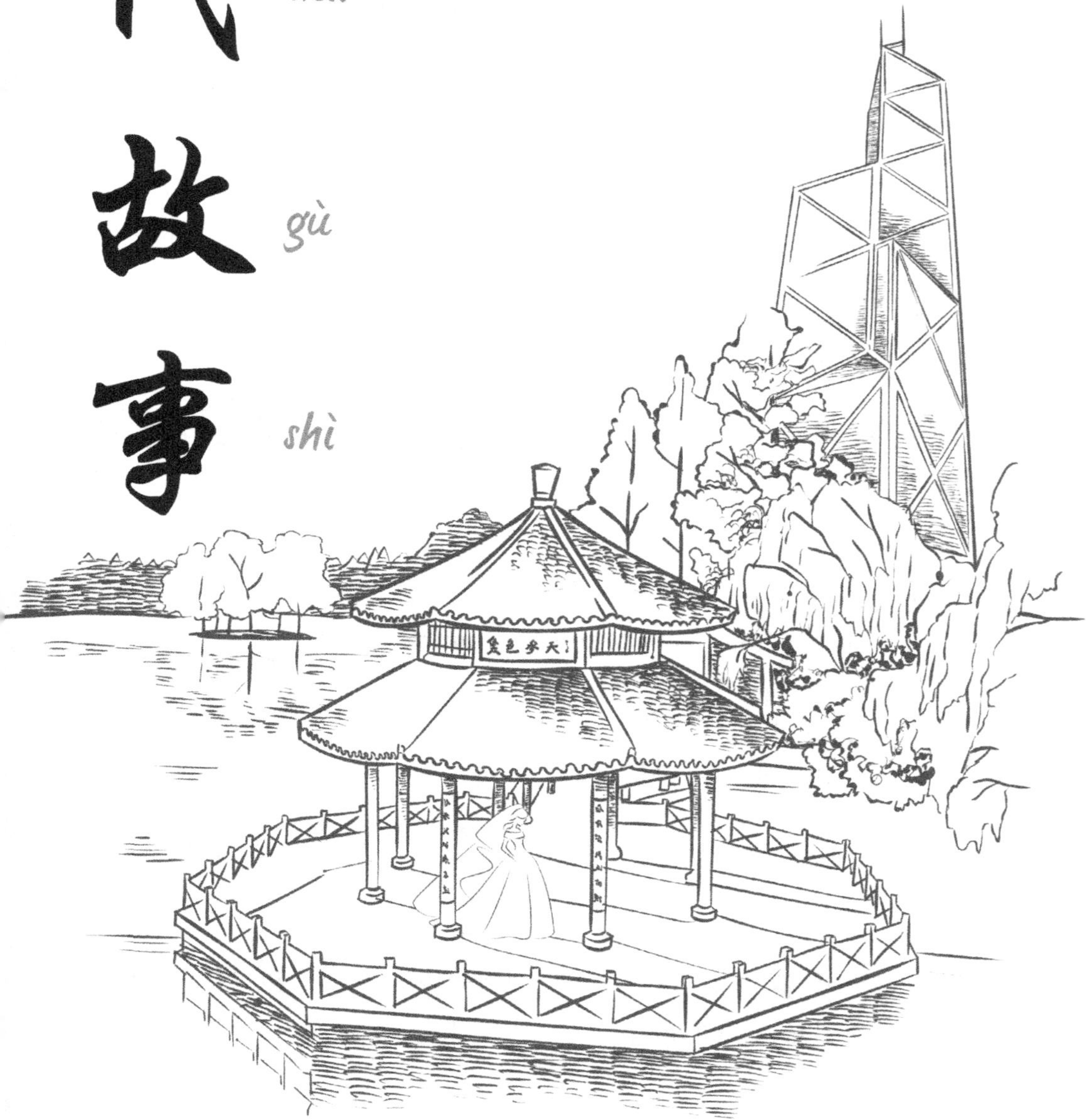

táo pǎo de xīn láng
逃跑的新郎
The Runaway Groom

wáng yǒng jīn nián èr shí sān suì, gāng gāng dà xué bì yè
王勇**今年**二十三岁，刚刚**大学**毕业。

Wang Yong is 23 years old **this year**, and just graduated from **university**.

yīn wèi tā yòu gāo yòu shuài, yòu yǒu qián, suǒ yǐ dà jiā jiào tā "gāo fù shuài"
因为他又高又帅，又有钱，**所以**大家叫他"高富帅"。

Because he is tall, handsome and rich, **so** everyone called him " the ideal man (tall, rich and handsome)."

tā yě shì dú shēng zǐ, fù mǔ fēi cháng ài tā
他也是**独生子**，**父母**非常爱他。

He is also an **only child**, so his **parents** love him very much.

zài tā shí bā suì de shí hòu, bà bà gěi tā mǎi le fáng zi
在他十八岁**的时候**，爸爸给他买了**房子**。

When he was eighteen years old, his dad bought him a **house**.

zài tā èr shí yī suì de shí hòu, tā jiù dāng shàng le jiā lǐ gōng sī de zhǔ guǎn
在他二十一岁**的时候**，他就当上了家里公司的**主管**。

When he was twenty-one, he already became the **director** of his family's company.

dà jiā dōu hěn xiàn mù tā, rèn wéi tā shì shì jiè shàng zuì xìng yùn de rén
大家都很**羡慕**他，**认为**他是**世界上**最幸运的人。

Everyone **envied** him, and **thought** that he was the luckiest person **in the world**.

kě shì zài xīn lǐ tā hěn bù kāi xīn
可是，**在心里**他很不开心。
However, **in** his **heart** he was very unhappy.

yīn wèi tā xiǎng chū guó liú xué dàn shì fù mǔ què ān pái tā jié hūn
因为，他想**出国留学**，但是父母却**安排**他结婚。
Because, he wanted to **study abroad**, but his parents **arranged** for him to get married.

xīn niáng yě shì gè yǒu qián rén yě shì tā fù mǔ zài yí cì xiāng qīn zhōng ān pái de
新娘也是个**有钱人**，也是他父母在一次**相亲**中安排的。
The **bride** is also a **rich person**, and was also arranged for him by his parents on a **blind date**.

wáng yǒng hé tā jiāo wǎng le bàn nián dàn shì bú ài tā
王勇和她**交往**了半年，但是不**爱**她。
Wang Yong **dated** her for half a year, but didn't **love** her.

tā jué de xīn niáng yào me ài tā de qián yào me ài tā de shuài
他觉得新娘**要么**爱他的钱，**要么**爱他的帅。
He felt that the bride **either** loved his money **or** his handsomeness.

kě shì wáng yǒng de fù mǔ gào sù tā ài qíng shì zàn shí de lì yì cái shì yǒng yuǎn de
可是，王勇的父母**告诉**他："爱情是**暂时**的，利益才是**永远**的。"
However, Wang Yong's parents **told** him: love is **temporary**, only benefits are **eternal**."

zài hūn lǐ nà tiān xīn niáng hé suǒ yǒu qīn qi péng yǒu dōu dào le dàn shì wáng yǒng méi dào
在**婚礼**那天，新娘和所有**亲戚朋友**都到了，但是王勇没到。
On the **wedding** day, the bride and all **family and friends** all arrived, but Wang Yong didn't arrive.

tā men děng le hěn jiǔ tū rán yí gè kuài dì yuán sòng lái le yì fēng xìn
他们等了**很久**，突然，一个**快递员**送来了一封**信**。
They waited for **a long time**, suddenly, a **postman** came to deliver a **letter**.

xiě zhe nǚ rén tài má fán wǒ zhǐ xiǎng dān shēn wǒ qù měi guó le zài jiàn
写着："女人太**麻烦**，我只想**单身**。我去**美国**了，再见！"
It read: "Women are too **troublesome**, I just want to be **single**. I'm on my way to the **USA**, goodbye!"

Culture Corner

In China, many parents try to intervene in their children's personal relationships and marriage. In ancient China, most marriages were arranged by parents, while it is no longer the case in modern days, it's still fairly common to see such conflicts. For rich families, this phenomenon can be even more common, as marriages are often seen as a means to establish mutual connections or benefits – just as in the famous Chinese idiom 门当户对 (mén dāng hù duì) (both the gates and the houses match), which means to be **well-matched in social and economic status for marriage**.

Wang Yong's parents told him:

ài qíng shì zàn shí de, lì yì cái shì yǒng yuǎn de.
爱情是暂时的，利益才是永远的。

Love is temporary, only benefits are eternal.

Do you agree? Why?

wǒ tóng yì / bù tóng yì, yīn wèi
我 同意 / 不同意，因为

I agree / disagree because

Key vocabulary

Pinyin	Chinese	Part of speech	English
dà xué	大学	*n.*	university
dú shēng zǐ	独生子	*n.*	only child
fáng zi	房子	*n.*	house
gāo fù shuài	高富帅	*slang*	the ideal man
zhǔ guǎn	主管	*n.*	director
xiàn mù	羡慕	*v.*	to envy
shì jiè	世界	*n.*	world
chū guó liú xué	出国留学	*vp.*	to study abroad
qīn qi péng yǒu	亲戚朋友	*n.*	family and friends
xīn niáng	新娘	*n.*	bride
xīn láng	新郎	*n.*	groom
xiāng qīn	相亲	*n.* *v.*	blind date have a blind date
jiāo wǎng	交往	*v.*	to date/ get along
zàn shí	暂时	*adj.*	temporary
yǒng yuǎn	永远	*adj.*	forever
hūn lǐ	婚礼	*n.*	wedding ceremony
yǒu qián rén	有钱人	n.	rich person
kuài dì yuán	快递员	*n.*	postman

Sentence patterns

yīn wèi ... suǒ yǐ ...
因为 ... 所以 ...

because ... so ...

yīn wèi + cause + suǒ yǐ + result
因为 + *cause* + **所以** + *result*

yīn wèi tā yòu gāo yòu shuài, yòu yǒu qián, suǒ yǐ dà jiā jiào tā "gāo fù shuài"。
因为他又高又帅，又有钱，所以大家叫他"高富帅"。

Because he is tall, handsome and rich, so everyone called him "the ideal man (tall, rich and handsome)."

yào me ... yào me ...
要么 ... 要么 ...

either ... or ...

yào me + action 1 + yào me + action 2
要么 + *action 1* + **要么** + *action 2*

tā jué de xīn niáng yào me ài tā de qián, yào me ài tā de shuài。
他觉得新娘要么爱他的钱，要么爱他的帅。

He felt that the bride either loved his money or his handsomeness.

Chinese version

王勇今年二十三岁，刚刚大学毕业。

因为他又高又帅，又有钱，所以大家叫他“高富帅”。

他也是独生子，父母非常爱他。

在他十八岁的时候，爸爸给他买了房子。

在他二十一岁的时候，他就当上了家里公司的主管。

大家都很羡慕他，认为他是世界上最幸运的人。

可是，在心里他很不开心。

因为，他想出国留学，但是父母却安排他结婚。

新娘也是个有钱人，也是他父母在一次相亲中安排的。

王勇和她交往了半年，但是不爱她。

他觉得新娘要么爱他的钱，要么爱他的帅。

可是，王勇的父母告诉他：“爱情是暂时的，利益才是永远的。”

在婚礼那天，新娘和所有亲戚朋友都到了，但是王勇没到。

他们等了很久，突然，一个快递员送来了一封信。

写着：“女人太麻烦，我只想单身。我去美国了，再见！”

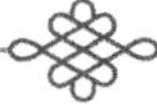

chūn tiān lái le

春天来了

Spring Has Come

lì lì de jiā zài nán fāng de yí gè nóng cūn
丽丽的家在**南方**的一个**农村**。
Lili's home is in a **village** in the **south**.

yì nián yǒu sì gè jì jié: chūn tiān, xià tiān, qiū tiān hé dōng tiān
一年有四个**季节**：春天，夏天，秋天**和**冬天。
There are four **seasons** in a year: spring, summer, autumn **and** winter.

lì lì zuì ài chūn tiān, yīn wèi chūn tiān zuì měi, dào chù dōu shì yīng huā shù
丽丽**最爱**春天，因为春天最美，**到处**都是樱花树。
Lili **loves** spring **the most**, because spring is the most beautiful, and there are cherry blossom trees **everywhere**.

lì lì yǒu sì gè xiōng dì jiě mèi: jiě jie、mèi mei、dì di, hé gē ge
丽丽有四个**兄弟姐妹**：姐姐、妹妹、弟弟，**和**哥哥.
Lili has four **siblings**: older sister, younger sister, younger brother, **and** older brother.

xiǎo de shí hòu, lì lì hé xiōng dì jiě mèi men guān xi hěn hǎo, cháng cháng zài yīng huā shù xià wán
小的时候，丽丽和兄弟姐妹们**关系**很好，常常在**樱花树**下玩。
When they were little, Lili had a good **relationship** with her siblings and they often played under the **cherry blossom tree**.

kě shì zhǎng dà hòu, tā men de guān xi biàn de shū yuǎn.
可是**长大**后，他们的关系变得**疏远**。

But after they **grew up**, their relationship became **estranged**.

xiōng dì jiě mèi men dōu qù le dà chéng shì, bú shì zuò shēng yì, jiù shì dāng bái lǐng.
兄弟姐妹们都去了大城市，**不是**做生意，**就是**当白领。

Her siblings all went to big cities, **either** doing business **or** being white-collar workers.

zhǐ yǒu lì lì, xuǎn zé liú zài nóng cūn péi fù mǔ.
只有丽丽，**选择**留在农村陪**父母**。

Only Lili **chose** to stay in the countryside to accompany her **parents**.

yǒu shí hòu, tā qù hé biān liù gǒu. yǒu shí hòu, tā qù tián lǐ zhòng shū cài.
有时候，她去河边**遛狗**。有时候，她去田里**种蔬菜**。

Sometimes she **walks** her **dog** by the river. Sometimes, she goes to the fields to **grow vegetables**.

yǒu shí hòu, tā zài yīng huā shù xià hé fù mǔ yì biān liáo tiān, yì biān hē chá.
有时候，她在樱花树下和父母一边**聊天**，一边**喝茶**。

Sometimes, she **drank tea** while **chatting** with her parents under the cherry blossom tree.

xiōng dì jiě mèi men kàn bu qǐ tā, rèn wéi tā zài nóng cūn bù néng zhèng dà qián.
兄弟姐妹们**看不起**她，**认为**她在农村不能**挣大钱**。

Her siblings **looked down on** her, **thought** that she cannot **earn much money** in the countryside.

zhí dào yǒu yì tiān, tā men tū rán zài yí gè shì pín píng tái shàng kàn dào tā.
直到有一天，他们突然在一个**视频平台**上看到她。

Until one day, they suddenly saw her on a **video platform**.

yuán lái, tā yì zhí zài pāi shì pín jì lù nóng cūn shēng huó.
原来，她一直在**拍视频**记录农村生活。

It turns out that she has been **shooting videos** to record village life.

tā xiàn zài bù jǐn yǒu jǐ bǎi wàn fěn sī, ér qiě yǒu hěn dà de shāng yè hé zuò.
她现在**不仅**有几百万粉丝，**而且**有很大的商业合作。

Now she **not only** has millions of fans, **but also** has a lot of business cooperation.

xiōng dì jiě mèi men dōu hěn chī jīng: chūn tiān lái le! zhè shì lì lì de chūn tiān!
兄弟姐妹们都很**吃惊**：春天来了！这是丽丽的**春天**！

Her siblings were very **shocked**: Spring has come! It's Lili's **spring**!

Culture Corner

In recent years, the Chinese internet has seen an explosion of content creators, **livestreamers** (主播 zhǔ bō), and **influencers** (网红 wǎng hóng). Similar to the west but the mainstream platforms in China are different, with the likes of Bilibili and TikTok (known as 抖音 dǒu yīn in China) being among the most popular.

Lili's siblings looked down upon her because they assumed she was making very little money, but now they know they were wrong, what do you think they will do?

A
jì xù shū yuǎn lì lì
继续疏远丽丽。
Continue to alienate Lili.

B
shēn qǐng jiā rù lì lì de shì pín tuán duì
申请加入丽丽的视频团队。
Apply to join Lili's video team.

C
xiàng lì lì dào qiàn, rán hòu gào sù tā: nǐ hěn bàng!
向丽丽道歉，然后告诉她：你很棒！
Apologize to Lili and tell her: You are awesome!

D
zhǔ dòng qīn jìn lì lì, rán hòu xiàng tā jiè qián
主动亲近丽丽，然后向她借钱。
Take the initiative to get close to Lili, and then borrow money from her.

Key vocabulary

nóng cūn 农村	*n.*	village	guān xi 关系	*n.*	relationship
chéng shì 城市	*n.*	city	shū yuǎn 疏远	*v.* *adj.*	to alienate estranged
jì jié 季节	*n.*	season	kàn bu qǐ 看不起	*v.*	to look down upon
dào chù 到处	*adv.*	everywhere	fù mǔ 父母	*n.*	parents
xiōng dì jiě mèi 兄弟姐妹	*n.*	siblings	liù gǒu 遛狗	*v.*	to walk dog
gē ge 哥哥	*n.*	older brother	liáo tiān 聊天	*v.*	to chat
dì di 弟弟	*n.*	younger brother	zhèng qián 挣钱	*vp.*	to earn money
jiě jie 姐姐	*n.*	older sister	shì pín 视频	*n.*	video
mèi mei 妹妹	*n.*	younger sister	fěn sī 粉丝	*n.*	fan/follower

Sentence patterns

bù shì jiù shì
不是 ... 就是 ...

either ... or ...

bù shì / **jiù shì**
不是 + *action 1* + **就是** + *action 2*

tā men bù shì zuò shēng yì, jiù shì dāng bái lǐng.
他们不是做生意，就是当白领。

They were either doing business or being white-collar workers.

bù jǐn ér qiě
不仅 ... 而且 ...

not only ... but also ...

bù jǐn / **ér qiě**
不仅 + *action 1* + **而且** + *action 2*

tā bù jǐn yǒu jǐ bǎi wàn fěn sī, ér qiě yǒu hěn dà de shāng yè hé zuò.
她不仅有几百万粉丝，而且有很大的商业合作。

She not only has millions of fans, but also has a lot of business cooperation.

CHINESE VERSION

丽丽的家在南方的一个农村。

一年有四个季节：春天，夏天，秋天和冬天。

丽丽最爱春天，因为春天最美，到处都是樱花树。

丽丽有四个兄弟姐妹: 姐姐、妹妹、弟弟，和哥哥。

小的时候，丽丽和兄弟姐妹们关系很好，常常在樱花树下玩。

可是长大后，他们的关系变得疏远。

兄弟姐妹们都去了大城市，不是做生意，就是当白领。

只有丽丽，选择留在农村陪父母。

有时候，她去河边遛狗。有时候，她去田里种蔬菜。

有时候，她在樱花树下和父母一边聊天，一边喝茶。

兄弟姐妹们看不起她，认为她在农村不能挣大钱。

直到有一天，他们突然在一个视频平台上看到她。

原来，她一直在拍视频记录农村生活。

她现在不仅有几百万粉丝，而且有很大的商业合作。

兄弟姐妹们都很吃惊：春天来了！这是丽丽的春天！

jiǎo cǎi liǎng zhī chuán
脚踩两只船
Dating Two at One Time

xiǎo yún shì dà xué lǐ de xiào huā, yòu cōng míng yòu piào liàng
小云是大学里的**校花**，又**聪明**又**漂亮**。

Xiaoyun is the **top beauty** at university, **smart** and **beautiful**.

nǚ shēng men jì dù tā, nán shēng men xǐ huān tā
女生们**忌妒**她，男生们**喜欢**她。

Girls are **jealous** of her, boys **like** her.

yīn wèi zhuī tā de nán shēng tài duō, tā bù zhī dào yīng gāi xuǎn zé shéi
因为**追**她的男生太多，她不知道应该**选择**谁。

Because too many guys are **chasing** her, she doesn't know who to **choose**.

píng ān yè dào le, xiǎo yún shōu dào le hěn duō píng guǒ lǐ wù, yǒu liǎng gè hěn tè bié
平安夜到了，小云收到了很多苹果**礼物**，有两个很**特别**。

Christmas Eve arrived, Xiaoyun received a lot of apple **gifts**, two of them were very **special**.

yí gè nán shēng wèi tā zhòng de dà hóng píng guǒ, hé lìng yí gè nán shēng gěi tā mǎi de píng guǒ shǒu jī
一个男生为他**种**的大红苹果，和**另一个**男生给她买的**苹果手机**。

One is a big red apple a guy **planted** himself for her, and **the other** is an **iPhone** (apple phone) another guy bought for her.

xiǎo yún dōu hěn xǐ huān, tā jiā le liǎng gè nán shēng de wēi xìn, kāi shǐ jiǎo cǎi liǎng zhī chuán.

小云都很喜欢，她加了两个男生的**微信**，开始**脚踩两只船**。

Xiaoyun liked both very much. She added the **WeChat** of two boys and started to **date both men at the same time** (feet step on two boats).

tā xiǎng xiān liǎo jiě tā men, zài jué dìng xuǎn shéi.

她想**先**了解他们，**再**决定选谁。

She wants to **firstly** get to know them separately, **then** decide who to choose.

yǒu yì tiān, xiǎo yún qí chē de shí hòu shuāi dǎo le.

有一天，小云**骑车**的时候**摔倒**了。

One day, Xiaoyun **fell off** while **riding a bike**.

tā de liǎn bèi huá shāng, liǎng gè nán shēng dōu qù yī yuàn kàn tā.

她的脸**被划伤**，两个男生都去**医院**看她。

Her face **got scratched**, and both guys went to the **hospital** to see her.

kě shì, nà gè sòng tā píng guǒ shǒu jī de nán shēng hěn kuài jiù zǒu le.

可是，那个送她**苹果手机**的男生很快就走了。

However, the guy who gave her the **iPhone** quickly left.

ér wèi tā zhòng píng guǒ de nán shēng liú xià le.

而为她种苹果的男生**留下**了。

Yet the guy who grew apple for her **stayed**.

tā gào sù tā: "bú yào dān xīn! wǒ huì zài zhòng yí gè píng guǒ. děng píng guǒ zhǎng dà le, nǐ jiù huī fù le."

他**告诉**她："不要**担心**！我会再种一个苹果。**等**苹果长大了，你就恢复了。"

He **told** her: "Don't **worry**! I will plant another apple (tree) for you. **When** the apple grows big, you will recover."

xiǎo yún hěn gǎn dòng, mǎ shàng qù bào tā, yīn wèi tā zhī dào yīng gāi xuǎn zé shéi le.

小云很**感动**，马上去**抱**他，因为她知道**应该**选择谁了。

Xiaoyun was very **moved**, and immediately **hugged** him, because she knew who she **should** choose.

Culture Corner

Although **Christmas** (shèng dàn jié 圣诞节) is not a public holiday in China, many companies and individuals celebrate it. Giving apples as gifts is a tradition on **Christmas Eve** (píng ān yè 平安夜) as the apple represents peace due to the words sounding similar in Chinese. Hence, apples are also called the fruit of peace on this day.

píng guǒ 苹果	píng ān 平安	píng ān guǒ 平安果
apple	peace	fruit of peace

"jiǎo cǎi liǎng zhī chuán
脚踩两只船" is Chinese slang for dating two people at the same time, literally meaning "feet step on two boats," which does sound quite dangerous! **Imagine if two attractive women/men both fancy you but you cannot decide whom to choose, will you date both at the same time, either secretly, or openly?**

A wǒ bù huì
我不会
I won't

B wǒ jué duì bù huì
我绝对不会
I absolutely will not

C wǒ kě néng huì
我可能会
Maybe I will

D wǒ dāng rán huì
我当然会
I definitely will

Key vocabulary

xiào huā 校花	*n.*	top beauty (school)	wēi xìn 微信	*n.*	WeChat
cōng míng 聪明	*adj.*	smart	qí chē 骑车	*v.*	to cycle/ride
piào liàng 漂亮	*adj.*	beautiful	shuāi dǎo 摔倒	*v.*	to fall off
jì dù 忌妒	*v.*	be jealous	yī yuàn 医院	*n.*	hospital
zhuī 追	*v.*	to chase	huī fù 恢复	*v.*	to recover
píng ān yè 平安夜	*n.*	Christmas Eve	dān xīn 担心	*v.*	to worry
lǐ wù 礼物	*n.*	gift	gǎn dòng 感动	*adj.*	moved/touched (emotionally)
tè bié 特别	*adj.*	special	bào 抱	*v.*	to hug
píng guǒ shǒu jī 苹果手机	*n.*	iPhone (apple phone)	yīng gāi 应该	*v.*	should/ought to

Sentence patterns

děng
等 …

when/at that time …

děng
等 + *subject* + *verb* + *clause*

děng píng guǒ zhǎng dà le, nǐ jiù huī fù le
等苹果长大了，你就恢复了。

When the apple grows big, you will recover.

bèi
… 被 …

indicate passivity (action placed upon)

bèi
subject + **被** + *verb* + *complement*

tā de liǎn bèi huá shāng
她的脸被划伤。

Her face got scratched.

Chinese version

小云是大学里的校花，又聪明又漂亮。

女生们忌妒她，男生们喜欢她。

因为追她的男生太多，她不知道应该选择谁。

平安夜到了，小云收到了很多苹果礼物，有两个很特别。

一个男生为他种的大红苹果，和另一个男生给她买的苹果手机。

小云都很喜欢，她加了两个男生的微信，开始脚踩两只船。

她想先了解他们，再决定选谁。

有一天，小云骑车的时候摔倒了。

她的脸被划伤，两个男生都去医院看她。

可是，那个送她苹果手机的男生很快就走了。

而为她种苹果的男生留下了。

他告诉她："不要担心！我会再种一个苹果。等苹果长大了，你就恢复了。"

小云很感动，马上去抱他，因为她知道应该选择谁了。

qǐ é jīn jīng

企鹅金晶

Penguin Jin Jing

zài nán měi zhōu yǒu yì zhī qǐ é měi nián yóu wǔ qiān yīng lǐ qù jiàn yí gè lǎo rén

在**南美洲**，有一只**企鹅**，每年游五千**英里**去见一个老人。

In **South America**, there is a **penguin** who travels 5,000 **miles** every year to see an old man.

zhè gè lǎo rén shì tā de ēn rén péng yǒu hé jiā rén

这个老人，是它的**恩人**、朋友、和**家人**。

This old man is its **rescuer**, friend, and **family** (member).

hěn duō nián qián zài bā xī de yí gè xiǎo dǎo yí gè lǎo rén zài hǎi biān bǔ yú

很多年前，在**巴西**的一个**小岛**，一个老人在海边**捕鱼**。

Many years ago, on a **small island** in **Brazil**, an old man was **fishing** by the seaside.

tū rán tā kàn jiàn le yì zhī qǐ é quán shēn shì hēi yóu yǎn yǎn yì xī

突然，他看见了一只**企鹅**，**全身**是黑油，**奄奄一息**。

Suddenly, he saw a **penguin** with black oil **all over its body**, and was **dying**.

tā jué de qǐ é tài kě lián le jiù mǎ shàng dài tā huí jiā

他觉得企鹅太**可怜**了，就**马上**带它回家。

He felt that the penguin was so **poor** that he **immediately** took him home.

tā bāng qǐ é xǐ qù le hēi yóu, tiān tiān wèi tā chī yú.
他帮企鹅**洗去**了黑油，天天**喂**它吃鱼。

He helped the penguin to **wash away** the black oil and **feed** him fish every day.

yì zhōu hòu, qǐ é huī fù le. qiáo ōu dài qǐ é qù hǎi biān, xiǎng sòng tā lí kāi.
一周后，企鹅**恢复**了。乔欧带企鹅去**海边**，想**送**它**离开**。

A week later, the penguin **recovered**. João took the penguin to the **seaside** and wanted to **send** him **away**.

kě shì, qǐ é què shě bu dé lí kāi, xuǎn zé liú xià péi qiáo ōu.
可是，企鹅却**舍不得**离开，选择**留下**陪乔欧。

However, Penguin was **reluctant** to leave and chose **to stay** to accompany João.

qiáo ōu wèi qǐ é qǔ míng "jīn jīng", měi tiān dài tā qù shā tān.
乔欧为企鹅**取名**"金晶"，每天带它去**沙滩**。

João **named** the penguin "Jin Jing" and took him to the **beach** every day.

tā men yì qǐ sàn bù, yì qǐ yóu yǒng, yì qǐ kàn rì luò.
他们一起**散步**，一起**游泳**，一起看**日落**。

They **walked** together, **swam** together, and watched the **sunset** together.

tā men shēng huó de hěn kāi xīn. kě shì jǐ gè yuè hòu, jīn jīng hái shì lí kāi le.
他们生活**得**很开心。可是几个月后，金晶**还是**离开了。

They lived happily. However, a few months later, Jin Jing **still** left.

qiáo ōu hěn xiǎng jīn jīng, cháng cháng huí yì tā men de kuài lè shí guāng.
乔欧很**想**金晶，常常**回忆**他们的**快乐时光**。

João **missed** Jin Jing very much, and often **recalled** their **happy times**.

yì nián hòu de yì tiān, qiáo ōu zhào cháng zài hǎi biān bǔ yú.
一年后的一天，乔欧**照常**在海边**捕鱼**。

One day a year later, João was **fishing** at the seaside **as usual**.

tū rán, tā tīng dào le yí gè shú xi de jiào shēng. tā tái tóu, kàn jiàn le tā de qǐ é jīn jīng.
突然，他听到了一个**熟悉**的叫声。他**抬头**，看见了他的**企鹅**金晶。

Suddenly, he heard a **familiar** call. He **looked up** and saw his **penguin** Jin Jing.

qiáo ōu hěn jī dòng, mǎ shàng qù bào jīn jīng, tā men zhōng yú tuán jù le.
乔欧很**激动**，马上去**抱**金晶，他们终于**团聚**了。

João was very **excited** and immediately went to **hug** Jin Jing. They were finally **reunited**.

hòu lái jīn jīng měi nián dōu huì huí lái kàn qiáo ōu jǐ gè yuè hòu yòu huì lí kāi
后来，金晶**每年**都会**回来**看乔欧，几个月后又会**离开**。

Afterwards, Jin Jing always **comes back** to see João **every year**, and would **leave** again after a few months.

qiáo ōu shuō jīn jīng jiù xiàng wǒ de hái zi tā shì bú huì wàng jì wǒ de
乔欧说："金晶就像我的**孩子**，它是不会**忘记**我的。"

João said: "Jin Jing is like my **child**, he will never **forget** me."

zhuān jiā men shuō jīn jīng shēng huó zài bā tǎ gē ní yà hǎi àn yào yóu wǔ qiān yīng lǐ cái néng huí dào qiáo ōu shēn biān
专家们说，金晶**生活**在巴塔哥尼亚**海岸**，要游五千**英里**才能回到乔欧身边。

Experts say that Jin Jing **lives** on the **coast** of Patagonia and has to swim 5,000 **miles** to get back to João's side.

yí lù shàng tā yào kè fú pí láo wēi xiǎn hé huài tiān qì
一路上，他要**克服**疲劳、**危险**，和坏天气。

Along the way, he has to **overcome** fatigue, **danger**, and bad weather.

kě shì jīn jīng què zài jiān chí yīn wèi tā hé qiáo ōu shì zuì qīn de jiā rén
可是，金晶却在**坚持**，因为它和乔欧是**最亲的**家人。

However, Jin Jing **carries on**, because he and João are the **closest** family.

SUMMARY

The Story of João and Penguin Jin Jing is a real story, traced back to 2011 when the 71-year-old Brazilian fisherman João rescued the injured penguin, and ever since they two developed such a strong bond that Jin Jing would swim 5000 miles to visit João every year! This story shows us that **compassion** (同情 tóng qíng), **kindness** (善良 shàn liáng) and **gratitude** (感恩 gǎn ēn) have no boundaries and should always be appreciated. The famous Chinese proverb "**滴水之恩当涌泉相报**" (dī shuǐ zhī ēn dāng yǒng quán xiāng bào) (**returning a favor many times more**) is perfectly displayed by penguin Jin Jing!

Which two characteristics do you think match Jin Jing and João the most?

wǒ jué de jīn jīng yòu
我觉得金晶又  又 
yòu

I think Jin Jing is ______ and ______

kě ài 可爱 *cute*	yǒng gǎn 勇敢 *brave*	fēng kuáng 疯狂 *crazy*	gǎn ēn 感恩 *thankful*

wǒ jué de qiáo ōu yòu
我觉得乔欧又 ______ 又 
yòu

I think João is ______ and ______

shàn liáng 善良 *kind*	yǒu tóng qíng xīn 有同情心 *compassionate*	hǎo wán 好玩 *fun*	kāng kǎi 慷慨 *generous*

Key vocabulary

qǐ é 企鹅	*n.*	penguin	wèi 喂	*v.*	to feed
yīng lǐ 英里	*n.*	mile	huī fù 恢复	*v.*	to recover
ēn rén 恩人	*n.*	saver/rescuer	hǎi biān 海边	*n.*	seaside
péng yǒu 朋友	*n.*	friend	shā tān 沙滩	*n.*	beach
jiā rén 家人	*n.*	family member	shě bu dé 舍不得	*v.*	to be reluctant
xiǎo dǎo 小岛	*n.*	small island	liú xià 留下	*v.*	to stay
bǔ yú 捕鱼	*v.*	to fish	lí kāi 离开	*v.*	to leave
yǎn yǎn yì xī 奄奄一息	*idiom*	dying	kè fú 克服	v.	to overcome
kě lián 可怜	*adj.*	poor	jiān chí 坚持	*v.*	to carry on

Sentence patterns

sòng lí kāi 送 ... 离开 ...

to send/see off

A + sòng 送 + *B* + lí kāi 离开

qiáo ōu xiǎng sòng tā lí kāi
乔欧想送它离开。

João wanted to send it away.

de ... 得 ...

to indicate result/degree

subject + *verb* + de 得 + *complement*

tā men shēng huó de hěn kāi xīn
他们生活得很开心。

They lived happily.

CHINESE VERSION

在南美洲，有一只企鹅，每年游五千英里去见一个老人。

这个老人，是它的恩人、朋友、和家人。

很多年前，在巴西的一个小岛，一个老人在海边捕鱼。

突然，他看见了一只企鹅，全身是黑油，奄奄一息。

他觉得企鹅太可怜了，就马上带它回家。

他帮企鹅洗去了黑油，天天喂它吃鱼。

一周后，企鹅恢复了。乔欧带企鹅去海边，想送它离开。

可是，企鹅却舍不得离开，选择留下陪乔欧。

乔欧为企鹅取名“金晶”，每天带它去沙滩。

他们一起散步，一起游泳，一起看日落。

他们生活得很开心，可是几个月后，金晶还是离开了。

乔欧很想金晶，常常回忆他们的快乐时光。

一年后的一天，乔欧照常在海边捕鱼。

突然，他听到了一个熟悉的叫声。 他抬头，看见了他的企鹅金晶。

乔欧很激动，马上去抱金晶，他们终于团聚了。

后来，金晶每年都会回来看乔欧，几个月后又会离开。

乔欧说：“金晶就像我的孩子，它是不会忘记我的”。

专家们说，金晶生活在巴塔哥尼亚海岸，要游五千英里才能到回到乔欧身边。

一路上，他要克服疲劳、危险，和坏天气。

可是，金晶却在坚持，因为它和乔欧是最亲的家人。

诗 shī

与 yǔ

爱 ài

情 qíng

Chinese Poetry with Love Stories

12

xiāng sī
相思

Yearning

hóng dòu shēng nán guó
红豆生南国
Red beans grow in southern land.

chūn lái fā jǐ zhī
春来发几枝
How many would sprout in spring?

yuàn jūn duō cǎi xié
愿君多采撷
Pick more for me, my dear friend.

cǐ wù zuì xiāng sī
此物最相思
As they bear our fond memory.

wáng wéi
王维
(701 - 761 AD)

Story

hěn jiǔ yǐ qián, yí gè nán hái hé yí gè nǚ hái xiāng ài le
很久以前，一个男孩和一个女孩**相爱**了。

A long time ago, a boy and a girl **fell in love**.

tā men cháng cháng shǒu qiān shǒu, qù hú biān sàn bù
他们常常**手牵手**，去湖边**散步**。

They often, **hand in hand**, went to the lake **to walk**.

hú biān yǒu yì kē hóng dòu shù, nán hái xǐ huān wèi nǚ hái zhāi hóng dòu
湖边有一颗**红豆树**，男孩喜欢为女孩**摘**红豆，

There was a **red bean tree** by the lake, and the boy liked **picking** red beans for the girl.

nǚ hái xǐ huān bǎ hóng dòu biān chéng shǒu liàn, tiān tiān dài zhe
女孩喜欢把红豆编成**手链**，天天**戴**着。

The girl liked weaving red beans into a **bracelet**, and **wore** it everyday.

zài shù xià, yǒu shí hòu, nán hái wèi nǚ hái chuī xiāo
在树下，有时候，男孩为女孩**吹箫**。

Under the tree, sometimes the boy **played flute** for the girl.

yǒu shí hòu, nǚ hái wèi nán hái tán qín
有时候，女孩为男孩**弹琴**。

Sometimes the girl **played zither** for the boy.

zài chūn fēng zhōng, tā men de ài qíng jiù xiàng hóng dòu, yòu měi hǎo yòu jiǎn dān
在**春风**中，他们的**爱情**就像红豆，又**美好**又**简单**。

In the **spring breeze**, their **love** is like the red bean, **beautiful** and **simple**.

rú guǒ shí jiān kě yǐ tíng zhǐ, tā men zhǐ xiǎng yǒng yuǎn zài yì qǐ
如果时间可以**停止**，他们**只**想永远**在一起**。

If time could **stop**, they **just** wanted to **be together** forever.

kě shì, yǒu yì tiān, nán hái yào qù hěn yuǎn de dì fāng, bù zhī dào shén me shí hòu néng huí lái
可是，**有一天**，男孩要去很**远**的地方，不知道什么时候能**回来**。

However, **one day**, the boy was going to a very **far** place, and didn't know when he would **come back**.

dì yī cì, nán hái kàn dào le nǚ hái de yǎn lèi
第一次，男孩看到了女孩的**眼泪**。

For the first time, the boy saw the girl's **tears**.

tā zǒu dào le hóng dòu shù xià, zhāi le yì kē hóng dòu, rán hòu, tā gào sù nán hái:

她**走到**了红豆树下，**摘**了一颗红豆，然后，她**告诉**男孩：

She **walked to** the red bean tree, **picked** a red bean, and then **told** the boy:

bù guǎn nǐ zài nǎ, wǒ de xīn dōu hé zhè kē hóng dòu yí yàng, yǒng yuǎn hé nǐ zài yì qǐ.

"**不管**你在哪，我的心**都**和这颗红豆一样，**永远**和你在一起。"

"**No matter** where you are, my heart will **always** be like this red bean, and will stay with you **forever**."

Culture Corner

This is a famous love poem from the Tang dynasty of China. "相思 (xiāng sī)" literally means "yearning". In Chinese culture, **red bean** (**红豆** hóng dòu) symbolizes love and yearning. Many Chinese people use it as a romantic love token, and in some traditional Chinese festivals, people would use red bean to make traditional desserts like **Red Bean Rice Balls** (**红豆汤圆** hóng dòu tāng yuán) for the good meaning of love and reunion.

Key vocabulary

xiāng ài 相爱	*v.*	to fall in love	jiǎn dān 简单	*adj.*	simple
shǒu qiān shǒu 手牵手	*vp.*	hand-in-hand	tíng zhǐ 停止	*v.*	to stop
hóng dòu 红豆	*n.*	red bean	zài yì qǐ 在一起	*vp.*	to be together
shǒu liàn 手链	*n.*	bracelet	yuǎn 远	*adj.*	far
dài 戴	*v.*	to wear (accessories)	yǎn lèi 眼泪	*n.*	tears
ài qíng 爱情	*n.*	romantic love	zhāi 摘	*v.*	to pick
měi hǎo 美好	*adj.*	beautiful/nice	bù guǎn 不管	*conj.*	regardless

Sentence patterns

hé yí yàng
… 和 … 一样

… the same as (like) …

A + **和** (hé) + *B* + **一样** (yí yàng)

wǒ de xīn hé zhè kē hóng dòu yí yàng
我的心和这颗红豆一样。

My heart is like this red bean.

bù guǎn dōu
不管 … 都 …

Regardless/no matter … will always …

不管 (bù guǎn) + *situation* + *subject* + **都** (dōu) + *result*

bù guǎn nǐ zài nǎ, wǒ de xīn dōu hé zhè kē hóng dòu yí yàng
不管你在哪，我的心都和这颗红豆一样。

No matter where you are, my heart will always be like this red bean.

CHINESE VERSION

很久以前，一个男孩和一个女孩相爱了。

他们常常手牵手，去湖边散步。

湖边有一颗红豆树，男孩喜欢为女孩摘红豆，

女孩喜欢把红豆编成手链, 天天戴着。

在树下，有时候，男孩为女孩吹箫。

有时候，女孩为男孩弹琴。

在春风中，他们的爱情就像红豆，又美好又简单。

如果时间可以停止，他们只想永远在一起。

可是，有一天，男孩要去很远的地方，不知道什么时候能回来。

第一次，男孩看到了女孩的眼泪。

她走到了红豆树下，摘了一颗红豆，然后，她告诉男孩：

“不管你在哪，我的心都和这颗红豆一样，永远和你在一起。”

rén miàn táo huā

人面桃花

A Charming Face Among Peach Blossoms

qù nián jīn rì cǐ mén zhōng
去 年 今 日 此 门 中
A year ago today by this gate,

rén miàn táo huā xiāng yìng hóng
人 面 桃 花 相 映 红
I saw your charming face among peach blossoms;

rén miàn bù zhī hé chù qù
人 面 不 知 何 处 去
Now I came again, but not being able to seeing you,

táo huā yī jiù xiào chūn fēng
桃 花 依 旧 笑 春 风
Only peach blossoms flying in the spring wind.

cuī hù
崔 护
(772—846 AD)

Story

táng cháo shí qī, nián qīng shī rén cuī hù zài jiāo wài sàn bù

唐朝时期，年轻**诗人**崔护在**郊外**散步。

During the **Tang Dynasty**, the young **poet** Cui Hu took a walk in the **suburbs**.

tā kàn dào le yí piàn táo huā lín, lǐ miàn yǒu yì jiān zhú wū

他看到了一片**桃花林**，**里面**有一间竹屋。

He saw a **peach blossom woods** with a bamboo house **inside**.

tā hěn hào qí, jiù qù qiāo mén. rán hòu, mén kāi le, yí gè hěn měi de nǚ hái zǒu le chū lái

他很**好奇**，就去**敲门**。然后，门开了，一个很美的女孩**走了出来**。

He was **curious** and went to **knock on the door**. Then, the door opened, and a beautiful girl **walked out**.

cuī hù hěn hài xiū, jiù shuō: qǐng wèn, nǐ kě yǐ gěi wǒ yì bēi shuǐ ma

崔护很**害羞**，就说："**请问**，你可以给我**一杯**水吗？"

Cui Hu was very **shy** and said, "**Excuse me,** could you give me **a cup of** water?

nà gè nǚ hái jiù xiào le yí xià, jiù qù gěi tā dào le yì bēi shuǐ

那个女孩就**笑了一下**，就去给他**倒**了一杯水。

The girl just **smiled a bit**, then went to **pour** him a cup of water.

cuī hù lí kāi hòu, yì zhí xiǎng zhe nǚ hái hé tā de táo huā lín

崔护**离开**后，一直**想着**女孩和她的桃花林。

After Cui Hu **left**, he kept **thinking** about the girl and her peach blossom woods.

yì nián hòu de chūn tiān, cuī hù yòu lái dào zhè lǐ

一年后的**春天**，崔护**又**来到这里。

One year later in **Spring**, Cui Hu came here **again**.

kě shì, mén shì suǒ shàng de, zhú wū lǐ méi yǒu rén

可是，门是**锁上**的，**竹屋**里没有人。

However, the door is **locked** and there was no one in the **bamboo house**.

tā xīn lǐ mǎn shì xiāng sī, jiù zài mén shàng xiě xià zhè shǒu shī

他心里**满是相思**，就**在门上**写下这首诗：

His heart was **full of yearning**, so he wrote down a poem **on the door**:

qù nián jīn rì cǐ mén zhōng

"去年今日此门中，

"A year ago today by this gate,

rén miàn táo huā xiāng yìng hóng
人面桃花相映红；

I saw your charming face among peach blossoms;

rén miàn bù zhī hé chù qù
人面不知何处去，

Now I came again, but not being able to seeing you,

táo huā yī jiù xiào chūn fēng
桃花依旧笑春风。”

Only peach blossoms flying in the spring wind.”

jǐ tiān hòu tā yòu lái dào zhè lǐ zhè cì tā gāo xìng de fā xiàn mén shì kāi de
几天后，他**又**来到这里。这次，他高兴地**发现**门是开的。

A few days later, he came here **again**. This time, he was pleased to **find** that the door was open.

kě shì tā jìn qù hòu zhī kàn dào le nǚ hái de fù qīn
可是，他**进去**后只看到了女孩的**父亲**。

However, after he **went in** he only saw the girl’s **father**.

fù qīn shuō nǚ hái kàn dào shī hòu dé le xiāng sī bìng yì zhí kū gāng gāng sǐ le
父亲说女孩看到诗后，得了**相思病**，一直哭，刚刚**死了**。

The father said that after the girl saw the poem, she got **lovesick** and kept crying, and just **died**.

cuī hù shāng xīn jí le tā mǎ shàng pǎo jìn fáng jiān bào zhe nǚ hái kū le
崔护伤心**极了**，他马上**跑进**房间，抱着女孩**哭**了。

Cui Hu was **extremely** heartbroken that he immediately **ran into** the room, hugged the girl and **cried**.

kě shì nǚ hái què tū rán xǐng lái yuán lái tā méi yǒu sǐ zhǐ shì hūn le
可是，女孩却突然**醒来**。**原来**，她没有死，只是**昏了**。

However, the girl **woke up** suddenly. **It turned out** that she was not dead, but **fainted**.

nǚ hái kàn dào le cuī hù tā kāi xīn de shuō táo huā kāi le nǐ zhōng yú lái le
女孩看到了崔护，她**开心**地说：桃花开了，你**终于**来了。

When the girl saw Cui Hu, she said **happily**: The peach blossoms are blooming, and you’ve **finally** come.

cuī hù yòu jī dòng yòu gǎn dòng, tā jué dìng bú zài lí kāi nǚ hái le
崔护又**激动**又**感动**，他**决定**不再**离开**女孩了。

Cui Hu was **excited** and **moved**, and he **decided** not to **leave** the girl anymore.

jǐ gè yuè hòu tā men jié hūn le, yì shēng dōu hěn xiāng ài
几个月后他们**结婚**了，**一生**都很相爱。

They **got married** a few months later and were very in love for the **rest of their lives** (whole life).

Culture Corner

This is one of the most renowned love poems in Tang dynasty, not only because its writing is so beautiful, but also because it recorded the true love story of the poet and the girl he loved. The most touching and beautiful poems are always driven by the deepest love and emotions. Later, the poem title "**人面桃花** (rén miàn táo huā)" (A Charming Face Among Peach Blossoms) also became a Chinese idiom, referring to "**recalling the beautiful memories of loved ones**."

Key vocabulary

Pinyin	Chinese	Part of speech	Meaning	Pinyin	Chinese	Part of speech	Meaning
shī rén	诗人	*n.*	poet	suǒ shàng	锁上	*v.*	to lock
jiāo wài	郊外	*n.*	suburbs	fù qīn	父亲	*n.*	father
táo huā	桃花	*n.*	peach blossoms	xiāng sī bìng	相思病	*n.*	lovesick
hào qí	好奇	*adj.*	curious	shāng xīn	伤心	*adj.*	sad/ heartbroken
qiāo mén	敲门	*v.*	to knock the door	kāi xīn	开心	*adj.*	happy
hài xiū	害羞	*adj.*	shy	zhōng yú	终于	*adv.*	finally
lí kāi	离开	*v.*	to leave	jié hūn	结婚	*v.*	to get married
chūn tiān	春天	*n.*	spring	yì shēng	一生	*n.*	a whole life

Sentence patterns

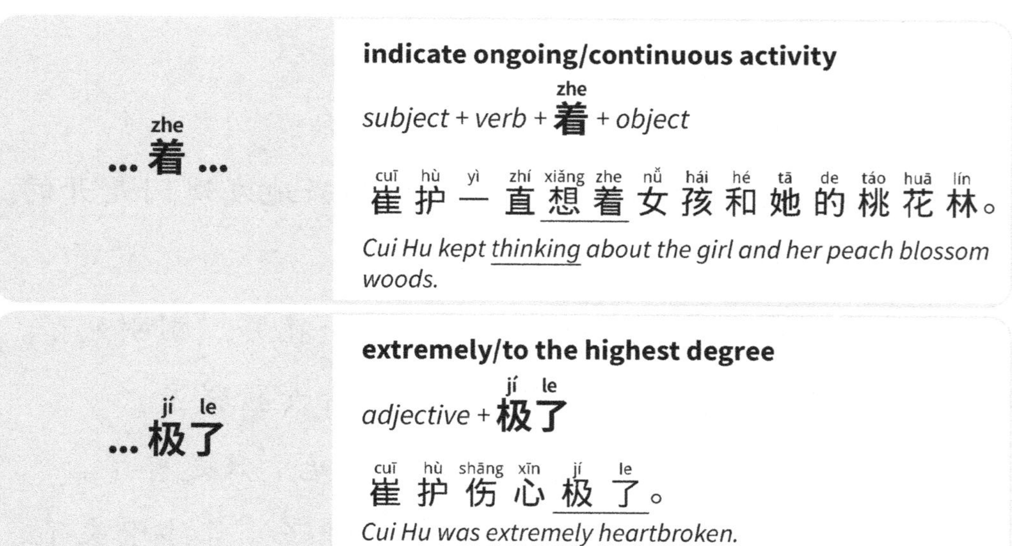

... 着 (zhe) ...

indicate ongoing/continuous activity

subject + verb + 着 (zhe) *+ object*

cuī hù yì zhí xiǎng zhe nǚ hái hé tā de táo huā lín

崔护一直想着女孩和她的桃花林。

Cui Hu kept thinking about the girl and her peach blossom woods.

... 极了 (jí le)

extremely/to the highest degree

adjective + 极了 (jí le)

cuī hù shāng xīn jí le

崔护伤心极了。

Cui Hu was extremely heartbroken.

CHINESE VERSION

唐朝时期，年轻诗人崔护在郊外散步。

他看到了一片桃花林，里面有一间竹屋。

他很好奇，就去敲门。然后，门开了，一个很美的女孩走了出来。

崔护很害羞，就说："请问，你可以给我一杯水吗？"

那个女孩就笑了一下，就去给他倒了一杯水。

崔护离开后，一直想着女孩和她的桃花林。

一年后的春天，崔护又来到这里。

可是，门是锁上的，竹屋里没有人。

他心里满是相思，就在门上写下这首诗：

去年今日此门中，

人面桃花相映红；

人面不知何处去？

桃花依旧笑春风 。

几天后，他又来到了这里。这次，他高兴地发现门是开的。

可是，他进去后只看到了女孩的父亲。

父亲说女孩看到诗后，得了相思病，一直哭，刚刚死了。

崔护伤心极了，他马上跑进房间，抱着女孩哭了。

可是，女孩却突然醒来。原来，她没有死，只是昏了。

女孩看到了崔护，她开心地说：桃花开了，你终于来了。

崔护又激动又感动，他决定不再离开女孩了。

几个月后他们结婚了，一生都很相爱。

成语故事

chéng yǔ gù shì

Chinese Idioms

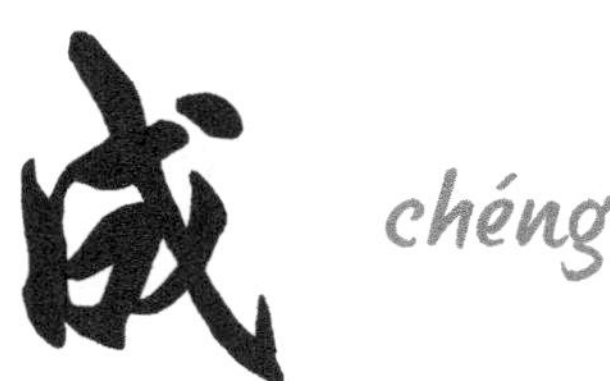

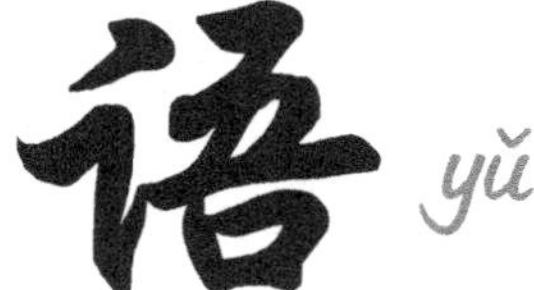

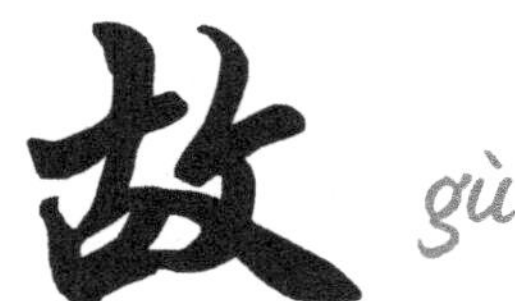

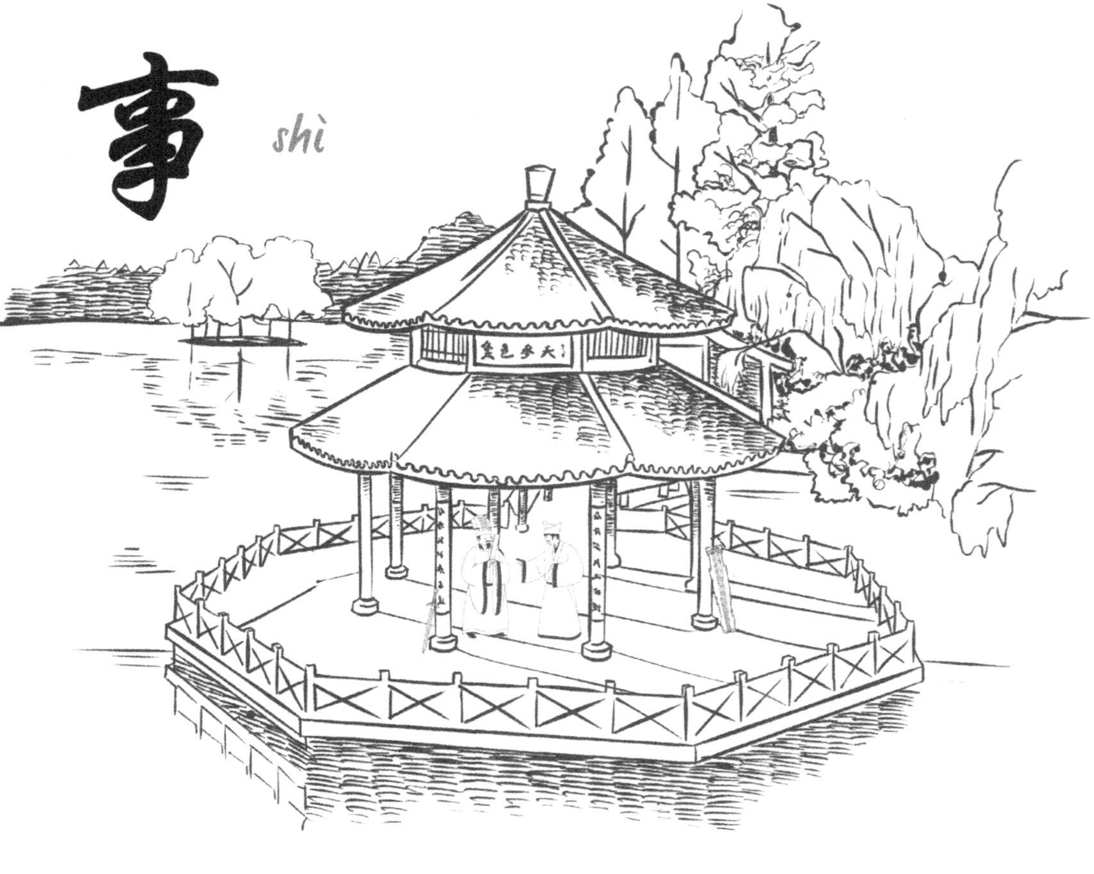

xiào lǐ cáng dāo

14 笑里藏刀

Hiding a Dagger Behind a Smile

zài táng cháo， yǒu gè guān yuán jiào lǐ yì fǔ。

在唐朝，有个**官员**叫李义府。

During the Tang Dynasty, there was an **official** named Li Yifu.

tā hé huáng dì de guān xi hěn hǎo。

他和**皇帝**的**关系**很好。

He had a good **relationship** with the **emperor**.

tā chángcháng hé tóng shì men shuō xiào， kàn shàng qù hěn yǒu hǎo， kě shì hěn huài。

他常常和**同事们**说笑，看上去很**友好**，可是很**坏**。

He often joked with his **colleagues**. He looked **friendly**, but was very **mean**.

tā xiào de yuè kāi xīn， jiù yuè huì zuò huài shì。

他笑得**越**开心，就**越**会做坏事。

The happier he laughed, the worse things he would do.

yǒu yí cì， tā tīng shuō jiān yù lǐ lái le yí gè xīn fàn rén， shì gè měi nǚ。

有一次，他**听说**监狱里来了一个新**犯人**，是个**美女**。

Once, he **heard** that a new **prisoner** had arrived in the prison, and was a **beautiful woman**.

tā jiù qù jiān yù bǎ fàn rén fàng le， rán hòu dài huí jiā dāng xiǎo lǎo pó。

他就去监狱**把**犯人放了，然后带回家当**小老婆**。

He went to the prison to release the prisoner, and then took her home to be one of his **side wives**.

tā de tóng shì bì zhèng yì zhī dào hòu, jiù qù gào sù tā bǎ fàn rén sòng huí jiān yù

他的**同事**毕正义知道后，就去告诉他**把**犯人送回监狱。

After his **colleague** Bi Zhengyi found out, he went to tell him to bring the prisoner back to the prison.

lǐ yì fǔ duì tā hěn kè qì, yì biān xiào, yì biān dā yìng

李义府对他很**客气**，一边笑，一边**答应**。

Li Yifu was very **polite** to him, **agreeing** while smiling.

kě shì, dì èr tiān, lǐ yì fǔ què qù jiàn huáng dì,

可是，第二天，李义府却去见**皇帝**，

However, the next day, Li Yifu went to see the **emperor**.

tā piàn huáng dì, shuō bì zhèng yì zuò le hěn duō huài shì, qǐng qiú chéng fá tā

他**骗**皇帝，说毕正义做了很多**坏事**，请求**惩罚**他。

He **lied to** the emperor and said that Bi Zhengyi had done a lot of **bad things** and asked to **punish** him.

huáng dì xiāng xìn le lǐ yì fǔ de huà, jiù liú fàng le bì zhèng yì

皇帝**相信**了李义府的话，就**流放**了毕正义。

The emperor **believed** Li Yifu's words and **exiled** Bi Zhengyi.

bì zhèng yì bù néng jiē shòu zhè gè dǎ jī, jiù zì shā le

毕正义不能**接受**这个**打击**，就**自杀**了。

Bi Zhengyi could not **accept** this **blow**, so he **committed suicide**.

hòu lái, hěn duō rén dōu shuō lǐ yì fǔ "xiào lǐ cáng dāo"

后来，很多人都说李义府"笑里藏刀"。

Later, many people all described Li Yifu as "hiding a dagger with a smile."

Summary

This is the orginal story behind the idiom 笑里藏刀 (xiào lǐ cáng dāo). It tells us that we need to stay alert and watch out those who appear friendly but are evil at heart. Sometimes, the greatest danger hides behind the most kind-looking face!

Learning Tip

笑里藏刀 (xiào lǐ cáng dāo) is a Chinese idiom, translated as: Hiding a Dagger with a Smile. It is used to describe those who appear friendly outside but with bad intentions inside.

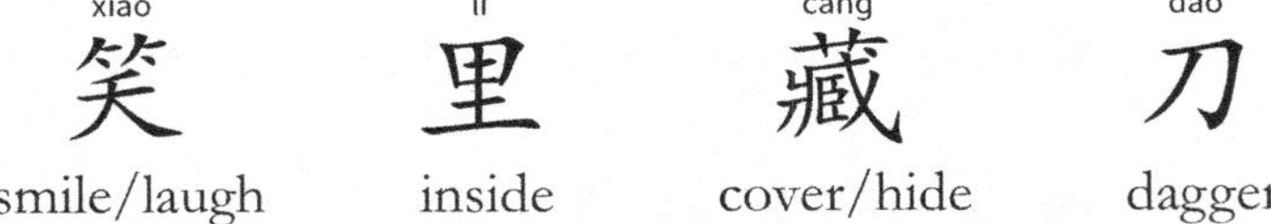

1 他是个笑里藏刀的人，你要小心。
(tā shì gè xiào lǐ cáng dāo de rén, nǐ yào xiǎo xīn.)
He is a man who **hides a dagger with a smile**, you have to be careful.

2 我发现他笑里藏刀后，就远离他了。
(wǒ fā xiàn tā xiào lǐ cáng dāo hòu, jiù yuǎn lí tā le.)
After I found out that he was **hiding a dagger with a smile**, I stayed away from him.

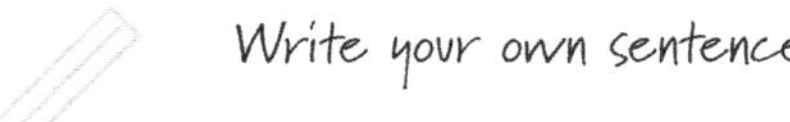

Key vocabulary

guān yuán 官员	*n.*	official	xiǎo lǎo pó 小老婆	*n.*	side wife
huáng dì 皇帝	*n.*	emperor	kè qì 客气	*adj.*	polite
guān xi 关系	*n.*	relationship	dā yìng 答应	*v.*	to answer
tóng shì 同事	*n.*	colleague	piàn 骗	*v.*	to lie
yǒu hǎo 友好	*adj.*	friendly	chéng fá 惩罚	*v.*	to punish
tīng shuō 听说	*v.*	to hear	xiāng xìn 相信	*v.*	to believe
měi nǚ 美女	*n.*	beauty	jiē shòu 接受	*v.*	to accept
fàn rén 犯人	*n.*	prisoner	dǎ jī 打击	*n.*	blow
jiān yù 监狱	*n.*	prison	zì shā 自杀	*v.*	to commit suicide

Sentence patterns

yuè yuè
越 … 越 …

the more … the more …

yuè yuè
越 + *action 1* + **越** + *action 2*

tā xiào de yuè kāi xīn, jiù yuè huì zuò huài shì.
他笑得越开心，就越会做坏事。

The happier he laughed, the worse things he would do.

bǎ
把 …

describing a certain action/imperative sentence

bǎ
把 + *object* + *verb*

bǎ fàn rén fàng le.
把犯人放了。

Release the prisoner.

CHINESE VERSION

在唐朝，有个官员叫李义府。

他和皇帝的关系很好。

他常常和同事们说笑，看上去很友好，可是很坏。

他笑得越开心，就越会做坏事。

有一次，他听说监狱里来了一个新犯人，是个美女。

他就去监狱把犯人放了，然后带回家当小老婆。

他的同事毕正义知道后，就去告诉他把犯人送回监狱。

李义府对他很客气，一边笑，一边答应。

可是，第二天，李义府却去见皇帝，

他骗皇帝，说毕正义做了很多坏事，请求惩罚他。

皇帝相信了李义府的话，就流放了毕正义。

毕正义不能接受这个打击，就自杀了。

后来，很多人都说李义府“笑里藏刀”。

duì niú tán qín

对牛弹琴

Playing Music to a Cow

chūn qiū shí qī, yǒu gè yīn yuè jiā jiào gōng míng yí, shàn cháng tán qín。

春秋**时期**，有个**音乐家**叫公明仪，**擅长**弹琴。

During the Spring and Autumn **period**, there was a **musician** named Gong Mingyi who was **good at** playing the Qin (Chinese musical instrument).

tā měi cì tán qín, rén men dōu huì pǎo guò lái tīng。

他**每次**弹琴，人们都会**跑过来**听。

Every time he played the Qin, people would **run over** to listen.

dà jiā jué de méi yǒu shén me bǐ tā de yīn yuè gèng měi！

大家觉得**没有什么比**他的音乐更美！

Everyone thinks **there is nothing more** beautiful **than** his music!

yǒu yì tiān, tiān qì hěn hǎo, gōng míng yí dài zhe qín qù le tián yě。

有一天，**天气**很好，公明仪带着琴去了**田野**。

One day, the **weather** was very good, Gong Mingyi took his Qin to the **field**.

tā kàn dào yì tóu dà huáng niú zài chī cǎo, jiù xiǎng tán qín gěi niú tīng。

他看到一头**大黄牛**在吃草，就想**弹琴**给牛听。

When he saw a **big yellow cow** grazing, so he wanted to **play the Qin** to the cow.

yīn wèi tā jué de niú huì hé rén yí yàng xǐ huān tā de yīn yuè。

因为他觉得牛会**和**人**一样**喜欢他的音乐。

Because he felt that the cow would like his music **the same as** humans.

yú shì, tā kāi shǐ tán 。kě shì, tán le hěn jiǔ, niú hái shì jì xù chī cǎo。
于是，他开始弹。可是，弹了**很久**，牛还是**继续**吃草。

So, he started to play. However, after playing for a **long time**, the cow still **continued** grazing.

gōng míng yí bú fàng qì, yòu tán le xīn yīn yuè。
公明仪不**放弃**，又弹了新**音乐**。

Gong Mingyi didn't **give up**, and played new **music**.

dàn shì, niú hái shì duì tā de yīn yuè méi yǒu xìng qù。
但是，<u>牛还是**对**他的音乐**没有兴趣**</u>。

But, <u>the cow was still **not interested in** his music</u>.

yí gè nóng mín kàn dào le, jiù gào sù gōng míng yí: "xiān shēng, nín bú yòng zài tán le, niú bú huì xīn shǎng yīn yuè。"
一个**农民**看到了，就**告诉**公明仪："先生，您**不用**再弹了，牛不会**欣赏**音乐。"

A **farmer** saw it and **told** Gong Mingyi: "Sir, you **don't need to** play anymore, cows can't **appreciate** music."

rán hòu, nóng mín chuī kǒu shào, niú tīng dào le, jiù gēn tā huí jiā le。
然后，农民**吹口哨**，牛听到了，就**跟**他回家了。

Then, the farmer **blew the whistle**, the cow heard it and **followed** him home.

hòu lái, zhè jiàn shì biàn chéng le xiào huà, "duì niú tán qín" de gù shì yě chuán kāi le。
后来，这件事变成了**笑话**，"对牛弹琴"的**故事**也**传开**了。

Later, this incident became a **joke**, and the **story** of "playing music (qin) to a cow" **spread**.

Summary

This is the original story behind **对牛弹琴** (duì niú tán qín), it tells us that sometimes it is **useless** (**没用** méi yòng) to please or reason with those who would never understand or appreciate things you want them to. In daily life, this idiom is often used in telling jokes or expressing disappointment in such matters.

Learning Tip

对牛弹琴 (duì niú tán qín) is a Chinese idiom, translated as: Playing Music (Qin) to a Cow. It is used to describe wasting time and effort to please or reason with those who would never understand or appreciate.

to cow play Qin

1 跟他讨论，真是**对牛弹琴**！
gēn tā tǎo lùn, zhēn shì duì niú tán qín!
Discussing with him is really **pointless**!

2 你不要**对牛弹琴**了，反正她不在乎。
nǐ bú yào duì niú tán qín le, fǎn zhèng tā bú zài hu.
Don't **waste your time or effort**, she doesn't care anyway.

Write your own sentence

Key vocabulary

shí qī 时期	*n.*	period (of time)	hěn jiǔ 很久	*n.*	a long time
yīn yuè jiā 音乐家	*n.*	musician	jì xù 继续	*v.*	to carry on
yīn yuè 音乐	*n.*	music	fàng qì 放弃	*v.*	to give up
shàn cháng 擅长	*v.*	be good at	nóng mín 农民	*n.*	farmer
měi cì 每次	*n.*	every time	bú yòng 不用	*adv.*	need not
dà jiā 大家	*n.*	everyone	xīn shǎng 欣赏	*v.*	to enjoy/ appreciate
tiān qì 天气	*n.*	weather	chuī kǒu shào 吹口哨	*vp.*	to blow whistle
tián yě 田野	*n.*	field	xiào huà 笑话	*n.*	joke
yú shì 于是	*conj.*	hence/so	chuán kāi 传开	*v.*	to spread

Sentence patterns

méi yǒu shén me bǐ
没有什么比 ...

nothing can compare

méi yǒu shén me bǐ
没有什么比 + *object* + *adjective*

méi yǒu shén me bǐ tā de yīn yuè gèng měi
没有什么比他的音乐(更)美！

There is nothing more beautiful than his music!

duì méi yǒu xìng qù
对 ... (没)有兴趣 ...

(not) be interested in ...

duì méi yǒu xìng qù
A + **对** + *B* + (**没**) **有**) **兴趣**

niú duì tā de yīn yuè méi yǒu xìng qù
牛对他的音乐没有兴趣。

The cow was not interested in his music.

Chinese version

春秋时期，有个音乐家叫公明仪，擅长弹琴。

他每次弹琴，人们都会跑过来听。

大家觉得没有什么比他的音乐更美！

有一天，天气很好，公明仪带着琴去了田野。

他看到一头大黄牛在吃草，就想弹琴给牛听。

因为他觉得牛会和人一样喜欢他的音乐。

于是，他开始弹。可是，弹了很久，牛还是继续吃草。

公明仪不放弃，又弹了新音乐。

但是，牛还是对他的音乐没有兴趣。

一个农民看到了，就告诉公明仪："先生，您不用再弹了，牛不会欣赏音乐。"

然后，农民吹口哨，牛听到了，就跟他回家了。

后来，这件事变成了笑话，"对牛弹琴"的故事也传开了。

bàn tú ér fèi

半途而废

Giving Up Halfway

yǒu gè nián qīng rén jiào lè yáng zi, tā yǒu gè yòu piào liàng yòu cōng míng de qī zi

有个**年轻人**叫乐羊子，他有个又**漂亮**又**聪明**的妻子。

There was a **young man** named Le Yangzi, he had a **beautiful** and **smart** wife.

yǒu yì nián, tā lí kāi le qī zi, qù le hěn yuǎn de dì fāng xué xí

有一年，他**离开**了妻子，去了很远的**地方**学习。

One year, he **left** his wife and went to a far **place** to study.

tā bú zài jiā de shí hòu, qī zi jiù tiān tiān zhī bù

他不**在家**的时候，妻子就**天天**织布。

When he was not **at home,** his wife weaved cloth **every day**.

kě shì, yǒu yì tiān, lè yáng zi què tū rán huí jiā le

可是，有一天，乐羊子却**突然**回家了。

However, one day, Le Yangzi **suddenly** went home.

qī zi hěn chī jīng, jiù wèn tā: "wèi shén me tí qián huí jiā?"

妻子很**吃惊**，就问他："为什么**提前**回家？"

The wife was **shocked**, so she asked him, "Why do you return home **in advance**?

lè yáng zi shuō: "wǒ zài xué xí de shí hòu, hěn xiǎng jiā, suǒ yǐ huí lái le"

乐羊子说："我在**学习**的时候，很**想**家，所以**回来**了。"

Le Yangzi said: "When I was **studying**, I **missed** home, so I **came back**."

qī zi tīng dào tā de huà hěn shī wàng tā qù ná le yì bǎ jiǎn dāo
妻子**听到**他的话，很**失望**。她去拿了**一把剪刀**，
bǎ zhī hǎo de bù jiǎn chéng liǎng bàn
把织好的布**剪**成两半。

Upon hearing his saying, the wife was very **disappointed**. She went to get **a pair of scissors** and **cut** the cloth she wove into two halves.

tā shuō nǐ kàn zhè shì wǒ huā le hěn cháng shí jiān zhī de bù
她说："你看，这是我花了**很长时间**织的**布**。
yì jiǎn kāi bù jiù fèi le
一剪开，布**就**废了。

She said: "Look, this is the **cloth** I had spent a **long-time** weaving. But **as soon as** it's cut, the cloth became wasted.

nǐ xué le yí bàn jiù fàng qì jié guǒ hé zhè kuài bù shì yí yàng de
你学了一半就**放弃**，**结果**和这块布是一样的。"

If you **give up** your study half way, the **result** is the same as this cloth."

lè yáng zi tīng dào hòu jué de hěn duì tā hěn kuài lí kāi le jiā huí
乐羊子**听到**后，觉得很**对**。他**很快**离开了家，**回**
dào le tā de xué xiào
到了他的学校。

Upon hearing this, Le Yangzi felt that it was very **correct**. He left home **soon** and **returned to** his school.

jǐ nián yǐ hòu tā chéng gōng bì yè le
几年**以后**，他**成功**毕业了。

After a few years, he **successfully** graduated.

SUMMARY

This the original story behind the idiom 半途而废 (bàn tú ér fèi), it tells us if you want to be successful, you must not give up halfway, otherwise, the previous efforts will have been in vain and wasted.

Learning Tip

半途而废 (bàn tú ér fèi) is a Chinese idiom, translated as: Giving up Halfway. It is used to describe those who give up on the half way of reaching goals.

1 要学好中文，就不能半途而废！
yào xué hǎo zhōng wén, jiù bù néng bàn tú ér fèi!
To learn Chinese well, one can't **give up halfway**!

2 成功的人不会半途而废！
chéng gōng de rén bú huì bàn tú ér fèi!
Successful people don't **give up halfway**!

Write your own sentence

Key vocabulary

nián qīng rén 年轻人	*n.*	young people	xiǎng 想	*v.*	to miss
cōng míng 聪明	*adj.*	smart	shī wàng 失望	*adj.*	disappointed
lí kāi 离开	*v.*	to leave	jiǎn dāo 剪刀	*n.*	scissors
dì fāng 地方	*n.*	place	jiǎn 剪	*v.*	to cut
tiān tiān 天天	*n.*	everyday	bù 布	*n.*	cloth
chī jīng 吃惊	*adj.*	shocked	fàng qì 放弃	*v.*	to give up
tí qián 提前	*v.*	in advance	jié guǒ 结果	*n.*	result
huí lái 回来	*v.*	to come back	huí dào 回到	*v.*	to return to
xué xí 学(习)	*v.*	to study	chéng gōng 成功	*v.* *adj.*	to succeed successful

Sentence patterns

dào
... 到

indicate result of an action

verb + **dào 到**

lè yáng zi tīng dào hòu, jué de hěn duì.
乐羊子听到后，觉得很对。

Upon hearing this, Le Yangzi felt that it was very correct.

yǐ hòu
... 以后

after ... (to express sequence of events)

time + **yǐ hòu 以后** + *clause (events)*

jǐ nián yǐ hòu, tā chéng gōng bì yè le.
几年以后，他成功毕业了。

After a few years, he successfully graduated.

Chinese version

有个年轻人叫乐羊子,他有个又漂亮又聪明的妻子。

有一年，他离开了妻子，去了很远的地方学习。

他不在家的时候，妻子就天天织布。

可是，有一天，乐羊子却突然回家了。

妻子很吃惊，就问他："为什么提前回家？"

乐羊子说："我在学习的时候，很想家，所以回来了。"

妻子听到他的话，很失望。她去拿了一把剪刀，把织好的布剪成两半。

她说："你看，这是我花了很长时间织的布。一剪开，布就废了。

你学了一半就放弃，结果和这块布是一样的。"

乐羊子听到后，觉得很对。他很快离开了家，回到了他的学校。

几年以后，他成功毕业了。

huà shé tiān zú

画蛇添足

Adding Feet to a Snake

yì jiā yǒu qián rén jì zǔ xiān hòu, sòng le yì píng jiǔ gěi gōng rén men

一家有钱人**祭祖先**后，送了一瓶酒给**工人们**。

After a wealthy family **paid homage to ancestors**, they gave a bottle of wine to their **workers**.

gōng rén men jué de zhè píng jiǔ tài shǎo, bù xiǎng fēn bēi

工人们**觉得**这瓶酒太少，不想**分杯**。

The workers **felt** that the wine was too little, and didn't want to **share it by cups**.

zuì hòu, dà jiā tóng yì yì qǐ zài dì shàng huà shé, shéi xiān huà wán jiù néng dé dào zhěng píng jiǔ

最后，大家**同意**一起在地上画蛇，**谁**先画完就能得到**整瓶酒**。

In the end, everyone **agreed** to draw snakes on the ground together, **whoever** first finished drawing would get the **whole bottle of wine**.

yú shì, dà jiā ná qǐ shù zhī kāi shǐ huà. hěn kuài, yǒu gè rén jiù huà wán le

于是，大家拿起**树枝**开始画。很快，有个人就**画完了**。

So everyone picked up the **branches** to start drawing. Soon, one guy **finished his drawing**.

tā fā xiàn qí tā rén hái zài huà, jiù shuō: nǐ men tài màn, wǒ zài
他发现**其他人**还在画，就说："你们太**慢**，我再

huà liǎng zhī jiǎo, yě huì bǐ nǐ men kuài
画两只脚，也会**比**你们**快**。"

He found that **others** were still drawing, so he said, "You are too **slow**. I can add two feet, and will still be **faster than** you."

suǒ yǐ, tā mǎ shàng yòu ná qǐ shù zhī gěi shé huà jiǎo
所以，他**马上**又拿起树枝给蛇**画**脚。

So, he **immediately** picked up the branch again to **draw** feet on his snake.

kě shì zhè shí hòu, páng biān yǒu gè rén gāng gāng huà wán
可是这时候，**旁边**有个人**刚刚**画完。

However, at this time, someone **next to** him had **just** finished his drawing.

zhè gè rén mǎ shàng xuān bù yíng le, ná qǐ jiǔ píng kāi shǐ hē
这个人马上**宣布**赢了，**拿起**酒瓶开始**喝**。

This man immediately **declared** he won, he **picked up** the wine bottle and started **drinking**.

rán hòu, tā duì nà gè zuì xiān huà wán shé de rén shuō: shé běn lái
然后，他对那个**最先**画完蛇的人说："蛇**本来**

jiù méi yǒu jiǎo,
就没有脚，

Then, he said to the **first** guy who finished the drawing: "Snakes don't have feet **in the first place**,

nǐ huà jiǎo bù jǐn duō yú, hái làng fèi shí jiān
你画脚不仅**多余**，还**浪费**时间。"

by adding the feet, it's not just **unnecessary**, but also **wasting** time."

nà rén tīng dào hòu, fēi cháng hòu huǐ! dà jiā dōu xiào tā bù yīng gāi
那人听到后，非常**后悔**！大家都**笑**他不应该

huà shé tiān zú
"画蛇添足"。

After that person heard it, he **regretted** it very much! Everyone **laughed** that he shouldn't "add feet to the snake".

SUMMARY

This is the original story behind the idiom 画蛇添足 (huà shé tiān zú). It tells us that after completing the task, there is no need to do meaningless things, otherwise it is just wasting time and energy.

Learning Tip

画蛇添足 (huà shé tiān zú) is a Chinese idiom, translated as: Adding Feet to a Snake. It is used to describe those who keep doing pointless things to an already well-completed task or product.

huà	shé	tiān	zú
画	蛇	添	足
draw	snake	add	feet

1 xiàng mù yǐ jīng wán chéng le， méi bì yào huà shé tiān zú！
项目已经完成了，没必要**画蛇添足**！
The project has been completed, there is no need to **do extra pointless things**!

2 nǐ zhè yàng huà shé tiān zú， zhēn shì làng fèi shí jiān！
你这样**画蛇添足**，真是浪费时间！
You are **doing pointless tasks** like this, what a waste of time!

Write your own sentence

Key vocabulary

yǒu qián rén 有钱人	*n.*	rich people	huà 画	*v.*	to draw
zǔ xiān 祖先	*n.*	ancestors	jiǎo 脚	*n.*	foot/feet
gōng rén 工人	*n.*	worker	yíng 赢	*v.*	to win
tóng yì 同意	*v.*	to agree	shū 输	*v.*	to lose
shéi 谁	*n.*	who/whoever	xuān bù 宣布	*v.*	to declare
zuì hòu 最后	*n.*	in the end	běn lái 本来	*adv.*	originally/in the first place
qí tā rén 其他人	*n.*	others	duō yú 多余	*adj.*	unnecessary
màn 慢	*adj.*	slow	làng fèi 浪费	*v.*	to waste
kuài 快	*adj.*	fast	hòu huǐ 后悔	*v.*	to regret

Sentence patterns

wán … 完	**indicate completion of an action** wán le *subject* + *verb* + **完**（**了**） hěn kuài, yǒu gè rén jiù huà wán le 很快，有个人就画完了。 *Soon, one guy finished his drawing.*
bǐ … 比 …	**indicate comparison (former higher/greater than latter)** bǐ *A* + **比** + *B* + *adjective* wǒ yě huì bǐ nǐ men kuài 我也会比你们快。 *I will still be faster than you.*

CHINESE VERSION

一家有钱人祭祖先后，送了一瓶酒给工人们。

工人们觉得这瓶酒太少，不想分杯。

最后，大家同意一起在地上画蛇，谁先画完就能得到整瓶酒。

于是，大家拿起树枝开始画。很快，有个人就画完了。

他发现其他人还在画，就说："你们太慢，我再画两只脚，也会比你们快。"

所以，他马上又拿起树枝给蛇画脚。

可是，这时候，旁边有个人刚刚画完。

这个人马上宣布赢了，拿起酒瓶开始喝。

然后，他对那个最先画完蛇的人说："蛇本来就没有脚，

你画脚不仅多余，还浪费时间。"

那人听到后，非常后悔！大家都笑他不应该"画蛇添足"。

民间传说

mín jiān chuán shuō

Chinese Folktales

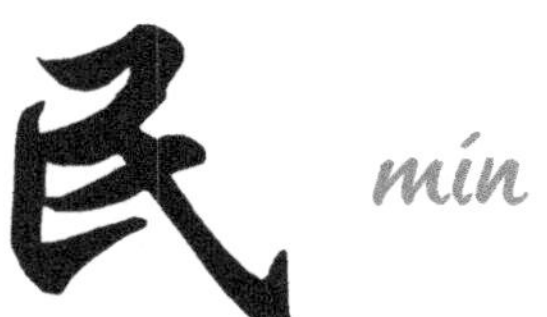

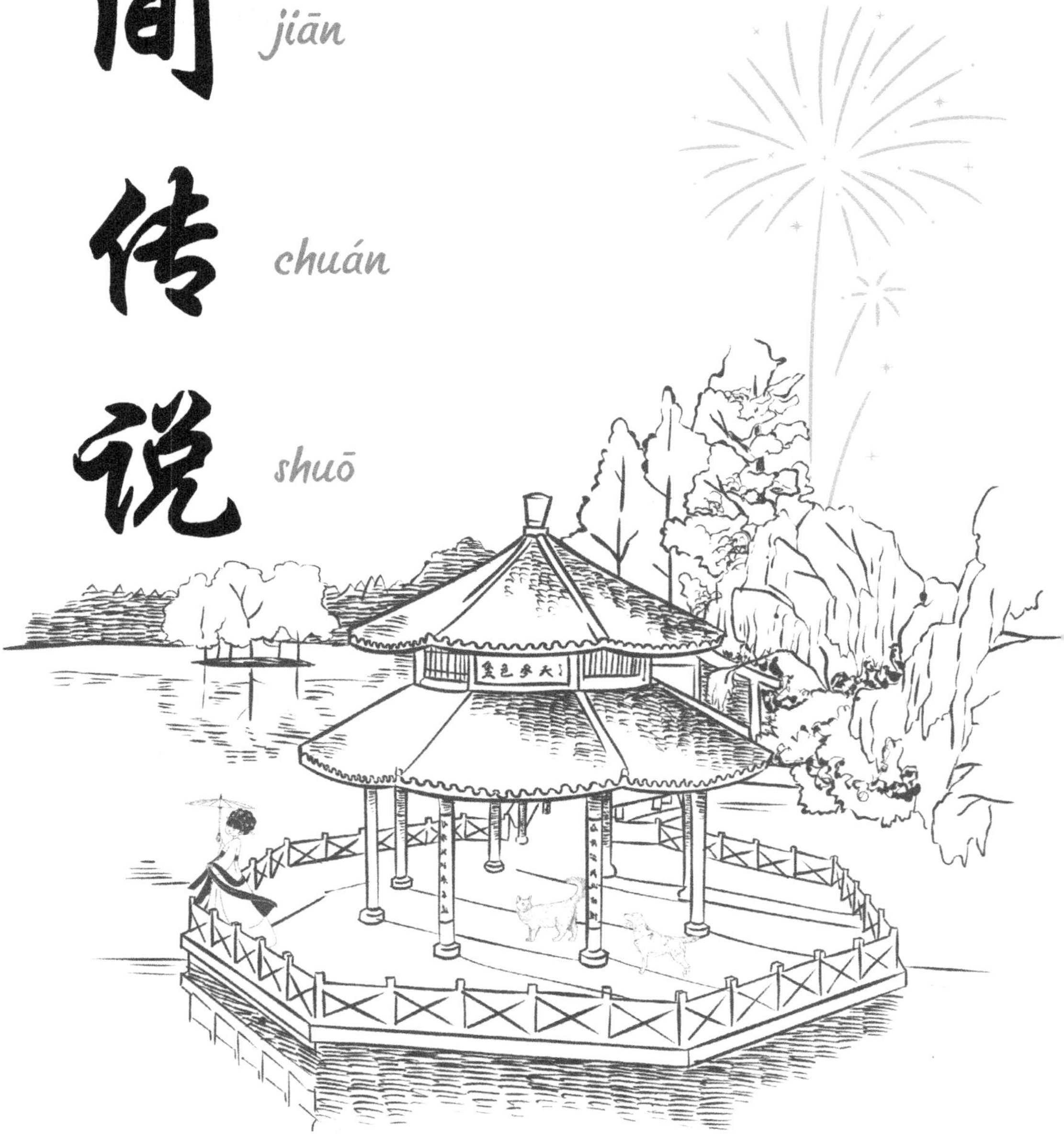

nián shòu

年兽

Legend of Beast Nian
(Chinese New Year Origin)

hěn jiǔ yǐ qián, sēn lín lǐ yǒu yì zhī guài shòu, jiào "nián", rén men jiào tā "nián shòu".
很久以前，**森林**里有一只**怪兽**，叫“年”，**人们**叫它“年兽”。

A long time ago, there was a **beast** living in the **forest** named "Nian" and **people** called him "Beast Nian".

tā yòu dà yòu chǒu, fēi cháng xiōng è, bù jǐn chī dòng wù, hái chī rén.
它又大又**丑**，非常**凶恶**，**不仅**吃动物，**还**吃人。

He was big, **ugly**, and very **vicious**, **not only** eating animals, **but also** people.

nián shòu měi cì lái cūn zi lǐ, huì chī hěn duō jiā qín.
年兽**每次**来村子里，会吃很多**家禽**。

Every time Beast Nian came to the village, he would eat a lot of **livestock**.

yǒu shí hòu, yì xiē lǎo rén hé hái zi yě huì bèi tā chī le.
有时候，一些**老人**和**孩子**也会被它吃了。

Sometimes, some **old people** and **children** would also be eaten by him.

hòu lái, rén men jiù kāi shǐ xiǎng bàn fǎ duì fu tā.
后来，人们就**开始**想办法**对付**它。

Later, people **began** to think of ways to **deal with** him.

rén men fā xiàn nián shòu shì měi sān bǎi liù shí wǔ tiān lái yí cì
人们**发现**年兽是每三百六十五天来**一次**，
People **found** that the Beast Nian came **once** every 365 days.

tā yì bān tiān hēi hòu dào tiān liàng qián zǒu ér qiě tā hěn pà biān pào
它一般**天黑**后到，**天亮**前走，而且它很**怕**鞭炮。
He usually arrived after **dusk** and leaving before **dawn**. And he was also **afraid of** firecrackers.

hòu lái rén men kāi shǐ suàn hǎo shí jiān měi dào zhè tiān wǎn shàng dōu huì tí qián chī fàn
后来，人们开始算**好**时间。每到这天**晚上**，都会**提前**吃饭。
Afterwards, people started to time it **well**. Every time that **night** arrived, they would eat meals **in advance**.

jiē zhe cáng hǎo jiā qín rán hòu fàng biān pào
接着**藏好**家禽，然后**放鞭炮**，
Then they would hide the livestock **well**, afterwards **set off firecrackers**,

zuì hòu guān shàng mén dāi zài jiā lǐ yì wǎn shàng dōu bú shuì jiào
最后关上门，**呆**在家里，一晚上都不**睡觉**。
Finally they closed the door and **stayed** at home without **sleeping** all night.

děng nián shòu dào le zhǎo bú dào huó wù yòu pà biān pào jiù lí kāi le
等年兽到了，**找**不到活物，又怕**鞭炮**，就**离开**了。
When Beast Nian arrived, he could not **find** a living creature, and was also afraid of **firecrackers**, so he **left**.

hòu lái zhè yì tiān jiù chéng wéi le zhōng guó rén de "nián sān shí" guò xīn nián jiù jiào "guò nián"
后来，这一天就**成为**了中国人的"年三十"，过**新年**就叫"过年"。
Afterwards, this day **became** the Chinese "New Year's Eve", celebrating **new year** is called "Passing Nian".

chī nián yè fàn fàng biān pào hé shǒu suì dōu chéng wéi le guò nián de chuán tǒng
吃**年夜饭**、放鞭炮和**守岁**都成为了过年的**传统**。
Eating the **New Year's Eve meal**, setting off firecrackers and **staying up late** all became **traditions** of the Chinese New Year.

Culture Corner

The legend of the Beast Nian is the original story of the **Chinese New Year** (新年 xīn nián), which occurs on the first day of the first month in lunar calendar. As it also marks the start of the Spring, so it is also called the **Spring Festival** (春节 chūn jié). The festival is the biggest festival event in China, with celebrations lasting for 2 weeks, ending with the Lantern Festival.

Have you celebrated Chinese New Year? **How many of the traditional activities below do you know?**

zài xīn nián, zhōng guó rén huì ______, ______ hé ______
在新年，中国人会 ______, ______ 和 ______

At Chinese New Year, Chinese people ______, ______ and ______

chī nián yè fàn 吃年夜饭 *have New Year's Eve meal*	fā hóng bāo 发红包 *send red packets*	fàng biān pào 放鞭炮 *release firecrackers*	fàng yān huā 放烟花 *release fireworks*	shǒu suì 守岁 *stay up late (for New Year's Eve)*
chī tuán yuán fàn 吃团圆饭 *have a reunion meal*	guà dēng lóng 挂灯笼 *hang lanterns*	chuān xīn yī 穿新衣 *wear new clothes*	bài nián 拜年 *pay a New Year's Visit*	tiē chūn lián 贴春联 *stick up spring couplets*

KEY VOCABULARY

sēn lín 森林	*n.*	forest	pà 怕	*v.*	be afraid
guài shòu 怪兽	*n.*	beast	tiān hēi 天黑	*n.*	dusk
chǒu 丑	*adj.*	ugly	tiān liàng 天亮	*n.*	dawn
xiōng è 凶恶	*adj.*	vicious	hòu lái 后来	*adv.*	afterwards
měi cì 每次	*n.*	every time	tí qián 提前	*v.*	in advance
jiā qín 家禽	*n.*	livestock	suàn 算	*v.*	to time/count
lǎo rén 老人	*n.*	old people	shuì jiào 睡觉	*v.*	to sleep
hái zi 孩子	*n.*	children	xīn nián 新年	*n.*	New Year
duì fù 对付	*v.*	to deal with/ counter	chuán tǒng 传统	*n.*	tradition

SENTENCE PATTERNS

bù jǐn hái 不仅 ... 还 ...

not only ... but also ...

bù jǐn hái
不仅 + *action 1* + **还** + *action 2*

tā bù jǐn chī dòng wù, hái chī rén.
它不仅吃动物，还吃人。

He not only eats animals, but also people.

hǎo ... 好

indicate successful completion of an action

hǎo
verb + **好** + *object*

rén men kāi shǐ suàn hǎo shí jiān.
人们开始算好时间。

People started to time it well.

CHINESE VERSION

很久以前，森林里有一只怪兽，叫“年”，人们叫它“年兽”。

它又大又丑，非常凶恶，不仅吃动物，还吃人。

年兽每次来村子里，会吃很多家禽。

有时候，一些老人和孩子也会被它吃了。

后来，人们就开始想办法对付它。

人们发现年兽是每三百六十五天来一次，

它一般天黑后到，天亮前走，而且它很怕鞭炮。

后来，人们开始算好时间。每到这天晚上，都会提前吃饭。

接着藏好家禽，然后放鞭炮。

最后关上门，呆在家里，一晚上都不睡觉。

等年兽到了，找不到活物，又怕鞭炮，就离开了。

后来，这一天就成为了中国人的“年三十”，过新年就叫“过年”。

吃年夜饭、放鞭炮和守岁都成为了过年的传统。

19

tián luó gū niang

田螺姑娘

The River Snail Maiden

cóng qián, yí gè nián qīng de dān shēn hàn zài hé biān jiǎn dào le yì zhī dà tián luó.

从前，一个年轻的**单身汉**在河边捡到了一只**大田螺**。

Once upon a time, a young **single guy** picked a **big river snail** by the riverside.

tā huí jiā hòu, bǎ tián luó yǎng zài shuǐ gāng lǐ.

他回家后，把田螺**养**在**水缸**里。

After he got home, he **kept** the river snail in a **water tank**.

tā bái tiān qù tián lǐ gàn huó, wǎn shàng duì tián luó shuō huà.

他**白天**去田里干活，晚上**对**田螺**说话**。

He went to work in the fields **in daytime** and **talked to** the river snail at night.

sān nián hòu de yì tiān, tā huí jiā hòu, tū rán kàn jiàn zhuō shàng yǒu zuò hǎo de fàn cài.

三年后的一天，他**回家**后，突然看见桌上有做好的**饭菜**。

One day three years later, when he **returned home**, he suddenly saw a prepared **meal** on the table.

tā cāi shì lín jū zuò de, jiù chī le.

他**猜**是**邻居**做的，就吃了。

He **guessed** it was made by the **neighbor**, so he ate it.

kě shì dì èr tiān tā huí jiā hòu yòu kàn dào le zhè xiē fàn cài
可是，**第二天**，他回家后**又**看到了这些饭菜。
However, **the next day**, he saw these meals **again** after returning home.

yú shì tā qù le lín jū jiā dào xiè kě shì lín jū què shuō bú shì tā men zuò de
于是，他去了邻居家**道谢**，**可是**，邻居**却**说不是他们做的。
So he went to the neighbor's house to **say thanks**, **however**, the neighbors (**yet**) said it was not them who did it.

tā jué de hěn qí guài kě shì xiǎng bu chū shì shéi zuò de
他觉得很**奇怪**，可是，**想不出**是谁做的。
He found it **strange**, but **couldn't think of** who did it.

zài hòu lái yí gè yuè tā měi cì gàn huó huí jiā dōu huì kàn dào zhè xiē hǎo chī de fàn cài
在**后来**一个月，他**每次**干活回家，**都**会看到这些**好吃**的饭菜。
In the **following** month, **every time** he came home from work, he would **always** see these **delicious** meals.

yì tiān tā gù yì tí qián huí jiā qiāo qiāo de cáng zài chuāng xià
一天，他**故意**提前回家，悄悄地**藏**在窗下。
One day, he went home early **on purpose** and **hid** quietly under the window.

hěn kuài tā kàn dào le nà tián luó tū rán biàn chéng le yí gè hěn měi de nǚ zi
很快，他看到了那**田螺**突然**变成了**一个很美的女子。
Soon, he saw that the **snail** suddenly **turned into** a very beautiful woman.

jiē zhe nǚ zi kāi shǐ zài chú fáng zuò fàn
接着，女子开始在**厨房**做饭。
Then, the woman started cooking in the **kitchen**.

tā jī dòng jí le mǎ shàng jìn qù bào nà nǚ zi dà shēng shuō yuán lái shì nǐ
他激动**极了**，马上进去**抱**那女子，**大声**说：原来是你！
He was **extremely** excited, and immediately went in to **hug** the woman, saying **loudly**: It was you!

nà nǚ zi hěn jǐn zhāng dàn chéng rèn le zì jǐ jiù shì nà zhī tián luó
那女子很**紧张**，但**承认**了自己就是那只田螺。
The woman was very **nervous**, but **admitted** that she was the snail.

yuán lái, tā yì zhí dān xīn nán rén bù néng jiē shòu zì jǐ, cái gù yì yǐn cáng.

原来，她一直**担心**男人不能**接受**自己，才故意**隐藏**。

It turned out that she kept **worrying** that the man could not **accept** her, so she deliberately **hid** it.

xìng yùn de shì, tā cuò le, yīn wèi nán rén yǐ jīng shēn shēn de ài shàng le tā.

幸运的是，她错了，**因为**男人已经**深深地**爱上了她。

Fortunately, she was wrong **because** the man already fell **deeply** in love with her.

hěn kuài, tā men jié hūn le, kāi shǐ xìng fú de shēng huó zài yì qǐ.

很快，他们**结婚**了，开始**幸福**地生活在一起。

Soon, they got **married** and started living **happily** together.

Culture Corner

The river snail maiden (田螺姑娘) is from the renowned Chinese folktale collection: **After Legend of the Demigods** (搜神记). It is one of the most loved romantic Chinese love stories with a rare happy ending. In ancient China, marriages were often arranged and free-will relationships were rare, yet such folktales revealed that despite this, the pursuit of true love still existed.

?

The river snail maiden received a happy ending because the man she loved willingly accepted who she really was. However, in reality, not everyone would choose this path. **If this story happened to you, what would you do with the snail maiden?**

A
ràng tā lí kāi
让她离开
Ask her to leave

B
ài tā hé tā zài yì qǐ
爱她，和她在一起
Love her and be together with her

C
hé tā zuò péng yǒu dàn shì bǎo chí jù lí
和她做朋友，但是保持距离
Be friends with her, but keep a distance

D
děi kàn qíng kuàng
得看情况
Depends on the situation

Key vocabulary

dān shēn hàn 单身汉	*n.*	single man	hǎo chī 好吃	*adj.*	delicious
tián luó 田螺	*n.*	river snail	chú fáng 厨房	*n.*	kitchen
bái tiān 白天	*n.*	daytime	jī dòng 激动	*adj.*	excited
wǎn shàng 晚上	*n.*	evening	jǐn zhāng 紧张	*adj.*	nervous
fàn cài 饭菜	*n.*	dishes/meal	chéng rèn 承认	*v.*	to admit
lín jū 邻居	*n.*	neighbour	yuán lái 原来	*adv.*	it turns out
dào xiè 道谢	*vp.*	to say thanks	yǐn cáng （隐）藏	*v.*	to hide
qí guài 奇怪	*adj.*	strange	jiē shòu 接受	*v.*	to accept
gù yì 故意	*adv.*	intentionally/ on purpose	ài shàng 爱上	*v.*	to fall in love with

Sentence patterns

kě shì què
可是 ... 却 ...

indicate contrary to the sentence before

kě shì què
可是 + *subject* + **却** + *verbal phrase*

kě shì lín jū què shuō bù shì tā men zuò de
可是，邻居却说不是他们做的。

However, the neighbors (yet) said it was not them who did it.

duì shuō huà
对 ... 说话

talk to

duì shuō huà
A + **对** + *B* + **说话**

tā wǎn shàng duì tián luó shuō huà
他晚上对田螺说话。

He talked to the river snail at night.

CHINESE VERSION

从前，一个年轻的单身汉在河边捡到了一只大田螺。

他回家后，把田螺养在水缸里。

他白天去田里干活，晚上对田螺说话。

三年后的一天，他回家后，突然看见桌上有做好的饭菜。

他猜是邻居做的，就吃了。

可是，第二天，他回家后又看到了这些饭菜。

于是，他去了邻居家道谢, 可是，邻居却说不是他们做的。

他觉得很奇怪，可是，想不出是谁做的。

在后来一个月，他每次干活回家，都会看到这些好吃的饭菜。

一天，他故意提前回家，悄悄地藏在窗下。

很快，他看到了那田螺突然变成了一个很美的女子。

接着，女子开始在厨房做饭。

他激动极了，马上进去抱那女子，大声说：原来是你！

那女子很紧张，但承认了自己就是那只田螺。

原来，她一直担心男人不能接受自己，才故意隐藏。

幸运的是，她错了，因为男人已经深深地爱上了她。

很快，他们结婚了，开始幸福地生活在一起。

māo gǒu bù hé

猫狗不和

The Original Break-up of Cats and Dogs

zài zuì kāi shǐ de shí hòu, māo hé gǒu shì hǎo péng yǒu

在**最开始**的时候，猫和狗是**好朋友**。

In the **very beginning**, cats and dogs were **good friends**.

hòu lái què xiāng hù tǎo yàn, shì yīn wèi fā shēng le yí jiàn shì

后来却**相互**讨厌，是因为发生了**一件事**。

But later, they disliked **each other**, all because of **one matter** that happened.

hěn jiǔ yǐ qián, yí gè jiào máo sān de nóng mín zài jiā lǐ yǒu yì zhī māo hé yì tiáo gǒu

很久**以前**，一个叫毛三的**农民**在家里有**一只猫**和**一条狗**。

A long time **ago**, a **farmer** named Mao San had **a cat** and **a dog** at home.

tā men shì hǎo péng yǒu, yì qǐ wán, yì qǐ kān jiā

它们是好朋友，一起**玩**，一起**看家**。

They were good friends, **playing** together and **looking after the house** together.

máo sān yǒu yì kē zhēn zhū. yì tiān, tā chū mén le, wǎn shàng yǒu gè zéi tōu le zhēn zhū

毛三有一颗**珍珠**。一天，他**出门**了，晚上有个**贼**偷了珍珠。

Mao San had a **pearl**. One day, he **went out**, and a **thief** stole the pearl at night.

māo hé gǒu yì qǐ zhuī, zéi pǎo de tài kuài, bǎ zhēn zhū diào jìn le hé lǐ

猫和狗一起**追**，贼跑得**太快**，把珍珠**掉进**了河里。

The cat and the dog **chased** together, the thief ran **too fast** and **dropped** the pearl **into** the river.

zhǔ rén máo sān jiù yào huí jiā le, māo hé gǒu hěn dān xīn。
主人毛三**就要**回家**了**，猫和狗很**担心**。
The owner Mao San was **about to** go home, and the cat and dog were very **worried**.

máo sān huí jiā hòu, zhēn de hěn shēng qì, mǎ shàng ràng tā men qù hé biān zhǎo zhēn zhū。
毛三回家后，**真的**很生气，**马上**让它们去河边**找**珍珠。
When Mao San got home, he was **truly** very angry and **immediately** asked them to go to the river to **find** the pearl.

tā gào sù tā men: shéi zhǎo dào zhēn zhū jiù néng chī ròu。
他**告诉**它们：**谁**找到珍珠就能吃肉。
He **told** them: **whoever** found it could eat meat.

yú shì, māo hé gǒu qù hé biān zhǎo le yì tiān。zuì hòu, māo zhǎo dào le zhēn zhū。
于是，猫和狗去**河边**找了一天。**最后**，猫找到了珍珠。
So the cat and dog went to the **riverside** and spent a day finding it. **Finally**, the cat found the pearl.

gǒu duì māo shuō: "wǒ men shì zuì hǎo de péng yǒu。yí huì ér zhǔ rén gěi nǐ ròu chī, nǐ yào liú yí kuài gěi wǒ。"
狗对猫说："我们是**最好的**朋友。**一会儿**主人给你肉吃，你要**留**一块给我。"
The dog said to the cat: "We are **best** friends. **In a while**, the master will give you meat, and you will **save** a piece for me."

māo dā yìng le。kě shì, zhǔ rén jiǎng lì ròu gěi māo de shí hòu, māo què bǎ ròu quán chī le。
猫**答应**了。可是，主人**奖励**肉给猫的时候，猫却把肉**全吃**了。
The cat **agreed**. However, when the master **rewarded** the cat with meat, the cat **ate all** the meat.

gǒu hěn shēng qì, jiù hé māo jué jiāo le。
狗很生气，就**和**猫**绝交**了。
The dog got very angry and **broke up with** the cat.

cóng cǐ, māo hé gǒu zài yě bú shì péng yǒu le, tā men yí jiàn miàn, jiù dǎ jià。
从此，猫和狗**再也不**是朋友了，它们一见面，就**打架**。
Since then, cats and dogs were **no longer** friends. As soon as they meet, they **fight**.

Culture Corner

The Original Break-up of Cats and Dogs (猫狗不和) is a classic Chinese folktale that tells us the origin discord between cats and dogs. If the cat was not greedy and was willing to share, he would not lose his dog friend. As for the dog, if he was tolerating and able to forgive, he would not lose his cat friend either. This story tells us that to maintain long-lasting friendships, we should treat our friends with **sincerity** (**真 诚**), **fairness** (**公 平**) and **tolerance** (**宽 容**).

In most cases, it is true that cats and dogs do not get on well. Do you also own a cat or dog? **From your experience, what do you think is the reason that they cannot get on well?**

A
māo hé gǒu shēng huó xí guàn bù tóng
猫和狗生活习惯不同
Cats and dogs have different living habits

B
māo hé gǒu xìng gé bù tóng
猫和狗性格不同
Cats and dogs have different personalities

C
māo hé gǒu xiāng hù jìng zhēng
猫和狗相互竞争
Cats and dogs compete with each other

D
māo hé gǒu tiān shēng xiāng hù tǎo yàn
猫和狗天生相互讨厌
Cats and dogs dislike each other by nature

KEY VOCABULARY

hǎo péng yǒu 好朋友	*n.*	good friend	zhǎo 找	*v.*	to find
xiāng hù 相互	*adv.*	each other	yú shì 于是	*conj.*	so/hence
yǐ qián 以前	*n.*	ago/before	zuì hòu 最后	*adv.*	finally
yǐ hòu 以后	*n.*	in future/after	hé biān 河边	*n.*	riverside
kān jiā 看家	*vp.*	to look after house	yí huì ér 一会儿	*n.*	in a while
zhēn zhū 珍珠	*n.*	pearl	dā yìng 答应	*v.*	to agree
chū mén 出门	*v.*	to go out	jiǎng lì 奖励	*v.*	to reward
zéi 贼	*n.*	thief	dǎ jià 打架	*v.*	to fight (physical)
zhuī 追	*v.*	to chase	chǎo jià 吵架	*v.*	to fight (verbal)

SENTENCE PATTERNS

jiù yào le **就要 ... 了**	**an event/action is about to happen** *subject* + jiù yào **就要** + *verb* + le **了** zhǔ rén máo sān jiù yào huí jiā le 主人毛三就要回家了。 *The owner Mao San was about to go home.*
hé jué jiāo **和 ... 绝交**	**to break up with** *(between friends)* *A* + hé **和** + *B* + jué jiāo **绝交** gǒu hé māo jué jiāo le 狗和猫绝交了。 *The dog broke up with the cat.*

CHINESE VERSION

在最开始的时候，猫和狗是好朋友。

后来却相互讨厌，是因为发生了一件事。

很久以前，一个叫毛三的农民在家里有一只猫和一条狗。

它们是好朋友，一起玩，一起看家。

毛三有一颗珍珠。一天，他出门了，晚上有个贼偷了珍珠。

猫和狗一起追，贼跑得太快，把珍珠掉进了河里。

主人毛三就要回家了，猫和狗很担心。

毛三回家后，真的很生气，马上让它们去河边找珍珠。

他告诉它们：谁找到珍珠就能吃肉。

于是，猫和狗去河边找了一天。最后，猫找到了珍珠。

狗对猫说："我们是最好的朋友。一会儿主人给你肉吃，你要留一块给我。"

猫答应了。可是，主人奖励肉给猫的时候，猫却把肉全吃了。

狗很生气，就和猫绝交了。

从此，猫和狗再也不是朋友了，它们一见面，就打架。

sān gè nǚ xù

三个女婿

Three Sons-in-law

zài yí gè zhōng qiū jié de wǎn shàng, yí wèi fù wēng qǐng tā de sān gè nǚ xù chī yuè bǐng
在一个**中秋节**的晚上，一位**富翁**请他的三个女婿吃**月饼**。

On the night of the **Mid-Autumn Festival**, a **rich old man** invited his three sons-in-law to eat **mooncakes**.

fù wēng xiǎng kǎo yí xià tā men de zhī shi shuǐ píng, jiù ràng tā men zuò shī
富翁想考**一下**他们的知识**水平**，就让他们**作诗**。

The old rich man wanted to **have a quick** test of their knowledge **level**, so he asked them to **compose poems**.

yāo qiú shì: shī zhōng yào yǒu "yuán yòu yuán"、"quē bàn biān"、"luàn zāo zāo"、"jìng qiāo qiāo"
要求是：诗中要**有**"圆又圆"、"缺半边"、"乱糟糟"、"静悄悄"。

The **requirement** was: the poem must **contain** the words of "round and round", "missing half", "messy", and "quiet".

dì yí gè nǚ xù shì gè lǎo shī, tā tái tóu kàn le yuè liàng, niàn dào
第一个**女婿**是个老师，他**抬头**看了月亮，念到：

The first **son-in-law** was a teacher, he **looked up** at the moon and read:

zhōng qiū yuè liàng yuán yòu yuán, guò le shí wǔ quē bàn biān;
"中秋月亮**圆又圆**，过了十五**缺半边**；

"The Mid-Autumn moon is **round and round**, after the fifteenth (day) it is **missing half**;

xīng xīng chū lái luàn zāo zāo, hēi yún gài yuè jìng qiāo qiāo."
星星出来**乱糟糟**，黑云盖月**静悄悄**。"

The stars came out in a **mess**, and the dark clouds **quietly** covered the moon."

fù wēng tīng le, shuō tā zuò de hěn hǎo.
富翁听了，说他**作**得很好。

The old rich man heard it and said it he **composed** very well.

dì èr gè nǚ xù shì gè chú shī, tā chī le yí kuài yuè bǐng, niàn dào:
第二个女婿是个**厨师**，他吃了一**块月饼**，念到：

The second son-in-law was a **chef**, he ate **a piece of mooncake** and read:

zhōng qiū yuè bǐng yuán yòu yuán, chī le yì kǒu quē bàn biān;
"中秋月饼**圆又圆**，吃了一口**缺半边**；

"Mid-Autumn mooncakes are **round and round**, with one bite it's **missing half**;

miàn shàng zhī má luàn zāo zāo, chī xià dù zi jìng qiāo qiāo."
面上芝麻**乱糟糟**，吃下肚子**静悄悄**。"

The sesame seeds on the flour are **messy**, and after eating, my stomach becomes **quiet**."

fù wēng xiào le yí xià, jué de yě kě yǐ.
富翁笑了**一下**，觉得也可以。

The old rich man smiled **a bit** and thought it was also okay.

dì sān gè nǚ xù shì gè tú hù, tā dōng kàn kàn, xī kàn kàn, rán hòu niàn dào:
第三个女婿是个**屠户**，他**东**看看，**西**看看，然后念到：

The third son-in-law was a **butcher**, he looked **east** and **west**, and then read:

yuè mǔ pì gǔ yuán yòu yuán, yuè fù sǐ le quē bàn biān;
"**岳母**屁股**圆又圆**，**岳父**死了**缺半边**；

"**Mother-in-law**'s butt is **round and round**, **father-in-law** is dead and **missing half**;

liǎng rén dōu sǐ luàn zāo zāo, quán jiā dōu sǐ jìng qiāo qiāo."
两人都死**乱糟糟**，全家都死**静悄悄**。"

Both died in a **mess**, the whole family died **quietly**."

gāng gāng shuō wán páng biān liǎng gè nǚ xù kāi shǐ dà xiào
刚刚说完，**旁边**两个女婿开始**大笑**。

After speaking, the two other sons-in-laws **next to** him **burst into laughter.**

fù wēng tīng le fēi cháng shēng qì jiù mà tā nǐ shì zuò shī hái shì zhòu wǒ
富翁听了非常**生气**，就**骂**他："你是作诗，还是**咒**我？"

The rich man felt very **angry**, and **scolded** him: "Are you composing poems or **cursing** me?"

nǚ xù fēi cháng bù hǎo yì si dàn tā zhī shi shuǐ píng zuì dī xiǎng bu dào gèng hǎo de
女婿非常**不好意思**。但他**知识**水平最低，**想不到**更好的。

The son-in-law was very **embarrassed**. But he has the lowest level of **knowledge** and **can't think of** anything better.

Culture Corner

Three Sons-in-law (三个女婿 sān gè nǚ xù) is a funny Chinese folktale. China has always taken pride in its beautiful poems and people often believe that a man's poem reveals its knowledge level. In ancient China, a man of great knowledge was always expected to be good at composing poems. In modern China, critics often enjoy using poems to express themselves and poetry competitions are popular activities in traditional festival events like the **Lantern Festival** (**元宵节** yuán xiāo jié) and **Mid-Autumn Festival** (**中秋节** zhōng qiū jié).

Which son-in-law's poems do you like the most and why?
You may choose from the below words to help to answer.

wǒ zuì xǐ huān 我最喜欢 *I like*	lǎo shī 老师 *(teacher)* chú shī 厨师 *(chef)* tú hù 屠户 *(butcher)*	de shī, yīn wèi 的诗，因为 *poem the most, because*	

yōu měi 优美 *beautiful*	làng màn 浪漫 *romantic*	yǒu yì si 有意思 *interesting*	hǎo wán 好玩 *fun*
yōu mò 幽默 *humorous*	gǎo xiào 搞笑 *funny*	tiáo pí 调皮 *naughty*	zhēn shí 真实 *realistic*

KEY VOCABULARY

Pinyin	Chinese		English	Pinyin	Chinese		English
zhōng qiū jié	中秋节	*n.*	mid-autumn festival	xiào	笑	*v.*	to smile/laugh
fù wēng	富翁	*n.*	old rich man	dōng	东	*n.*	east
yuè bǐng	月饼	*n.*	mooncake	xī	西	*n.*	west
zhī shi	知识	*n.*	knowledge	yuè mǔ	岳母	*n.*	mother-in-law (man's)
shuǐ píng	水平	*n.*	level	yuè fù	岳父	*n.*	father-in-law (man's)
yāo qiú	要求	*n.*	requirement	mà	骂	*v.*	to scold
nǚ xù	女婿	*n.*	son-in-law	zhòu	咒	*v.*	to curse
bù hǎo yì si	不好意思	*adj.*	embarrassed	yí kuài	一块		a piece of

SENTENCE PATTERNS

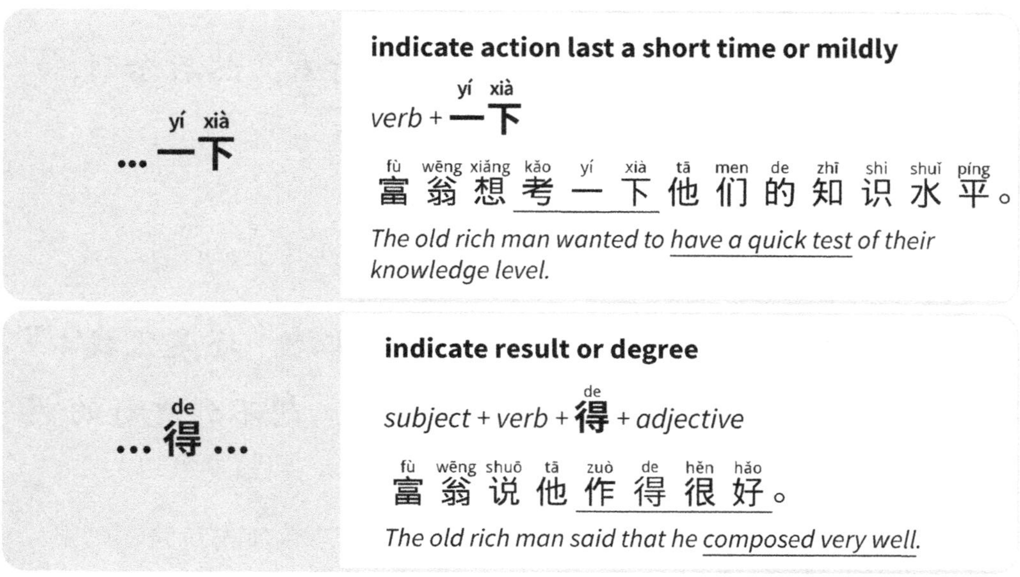

yí xià
... 一下

indicate action last a short time or mildly

verb + 一下 (yí xià)

fù wēng xiǎng kǎo yí xià tā men de zhī shi shuǐ píng
富翁想考一下他们的知识水平。

The old rich man wanted to have a quick test of their knowledge level.

de
... 得 ...

indicate result or degree

subject + *verb* + 得 (de) + *adjective*

fù wēng shuō tā zuò de hěn hǎo
富翁说他作得很好。

The old rich man said that he composed very well.

CHINESE VERSION

在一个中秋节的晚上，一位富翁请他的三个女婿吃月饼。

富翁想考一下他们的知识水平，就让他们作诗。

要求是：诗中要有　“圆又圆”、“缺半边”、“乱糟糟”、“静悄悄”。

第一个女婿是个老师，他抬头看了月亮，念到：

“中秋月亮圆又圆，过了十五缺半边；

星星出来乱糟糟，黑云盖月静悄悄。”

富翁听了，说他作得很好。

第二个女婿是个厨师，他吃了一块月饼，念到：

“中秋月饼圆又圆，吃了一口缺半边；

面上芝麻乱糟糟，吃下肚子静悄悄。”

富翁笑了一下，觉得也可以。

第三个女婿是个屠户，他东看看，西看看，然后念到：

“岳母屁股圆又圆，岳父死了缺半边；

两人都死乱糟糟，全家都死静悄悄。”

刚刚说完，旁边两个女婿开始大笑。

富翁听了非常生气，就骂他：“你是作诗，还是咒我？”

女婿非常不好意思。但他知识水平最低，想不到更好的。

jīn dòu zǐ hé lǎo gōng jī

金豆子和老公鸡 22

The Old Rooster and the Gold Bean

cóng qián yǒu gè kě lián de hái zi jiào zhù zi

从前，有个**可怜**的孩子叫柱子。

Once upon a time, there was a **poor** child named Zhuzi.

yīn wèi tā de fù mǔ sǐ le suǒ yǐ tā hé gē ge sǎo sao zhù zài yì qǐ

因为他的父母死了，**所以**他和哥哥嫂嫂住在一起。

Because his parents were dead, **so** he was living with his older brother and sister-in-law.

kě shì tā men bù jǐn tiān tiān ràng tā gàn zhòng huó hái qī fù tā

可是，他们不仅天天让他干**重活**，还**欺负**他。

However, they not only ask him to do **heavy work** everyday, but **bullied** him.

hòu lái gē ge sǎo sao ràng tā lí kāi zhǐ gěi le tā yì jiān pò fáng zǐ yí kuài xiǎo tián hé yì zhī lǎo gōng jī

后来，**哥哥嫂嫂**让他离开，只给了他一间**破房子**，一块小田和一只**老公鸡**。

Later, his **brother and sister-in-law** asked him to leave, only giving him a **broken house**, a small field and an **old rooster**.

zhù zi měi tiān zài tián lǐ nǔ lì gàn huó tā duì lǎo gōng jī hěn hǎo dàng tā shì jiā rén

柱子**每天**在田里**努力**干活。他对老公鸡很好，**当**它**是**家人。

Zhuzi **worked hard** on the field **every day**. He was very kind to the old rooster, **treating** it **as** a family member.

yì tiān lǎo gōng jī tū rán shuō huà gào sù zhù zi
一天，老公鸡突然**说话**，告诉柱子：

One day, the old rooster **spoke** suddenly and told Zhuzi:

qù bǎ wǒ de jī fèn zhòng zài tián lǐ néng zhǎng chū jīn dòu zǐ
"去把我的**鸡粪**种在田里，能长出**金豆子**。"

"Go and take my **manure** to plant in the field, and it can grow into **gold beans**."

zhù zi suī rán hěn chī jīng dàn tā zhào zuò le
柱子虽然很**吃惊**，但他**照做**了。

Although Zhuzi was **shocked**, but he **followed the instruction**.

jié guǒ jǐ tiān hòu tián lǐ zhēn de zhǎng mǎn le jīn dòu zi hěn zhí qián
结果，几天后田里**真的**长满了金豆子，很**值钱**。

As a result, after several days the field was **really** full of gold beans, **worth lots of money**.

gē ge sǎo sao tīng shuō le jiù qù zhù zi de jiā tōu le lǎo gōng jī
哥哥嫂嫂**听说**了，就去柱子的家**偷**了老公鸡。

The brother and sister-in-law **heard about** it, so they **stole** the old rooser.

tā men wèi le dé dào lǎo gōng jī de jī fèn yì zhí pāi dǎ lǎo gōng jī de pì gǔ
他们为了**得到**老公鸡的鸡粪，**一直**拍打老公鸡的**屁股**。

In order **to get** the old rooster's manure, they **kept** patting the old rooster's **butt**.

kě shì tā men pāi dǎ le jǐ tiān yě méi yǒu dé dào jī fèn
可是，它们拍打了**几天**，也没有得到鸡粪。

However, they pat for a **few days** without getting any chicken manure.

zhù zi fā xiàn lǎo gōng jī bú jiàn hòu fēi cháng zhāo jí dào chù zhǎo lǎo gōng jī
柱子**发现**老公鸡**不见**后，非常**着急**，**到处**找老公鸡。

When Zhuzi **found out** that the old rooster was **missing**, he was very **anxious** and looked for the old rooster **everywhere**.

zhōng yú zhù zi zhǎo dào le gē ge sǎo sao de jiā kàn jiàn tā men ná zhe dāo yào shā lǎo gōng jī
终于，柱子找到了**哥哥嫂嫂**的家，看见他们**拿着刀**要杀老公鸡。

Finally, Zhuzi went to the house of his **brother and sister-in-law** to look, and saw that they were **holding a knife** to kill the old rooster.

zhù zi lì kè qiǎng guò dāo jiù le lǎo gōng jī
柱子**立刻**抢过刀，**救**了老公鸡。

Zhuzi **immediately** grabbed the knife and **saved** the old rooster.

zhè shí lǎo gōng jī tū rán fēi qǐ lái zài gē ge sǎo sao de liǎn shàng pēn le jī fèn rán hòu hé zhù zi lí kāi le
这时，老公鸡突然**飞起来**，在哥哥嫂嫂的脸上**喷**了鸡粪，然后和柱子**离开**了。

At this moment, the old rooster suddenly **flew up**, **sprayed** manure on the faces of his brother and sister-in-law, and then **left** with Zhuzi.

gē ge sǎo sao lì kè qù xǐ liǎn dàn shì xǐ bu diào jī fèn
哥哥嫂嫂**立刻**去洗脸，但是**洗不掉**鸡粪。

The brother and sister-in-law **immediately** went to wash their faces, but they **couldn't wash away** the chicken manure.

ér jī fèn yě méi biàn chéng jīn dòu zi tā men bù hǎo yì si jiàn rén cóng cǐ bú zài chū mén le
而鸡粪也没**变成**金豆子，他们**不好意思**见人，从此不再**出门**了。

And the chicken manure didn't **turn into** golden beans. They were **embarrassed** to meet people and from then never **went out** again.

Culture Corner

The Old Rooster and the Gold Bean (jīn dòu zi hé lǎo gōng jī 金豆子和老公鸡) is a classic Chinese folktale. **Respecting the old and loving the young** (zūn lǎo ài yòu **尊老爱幼**) is a traditional concept of Chinese Confucianism. Those who abide by this concept are praised, and those who don't are punished, which is what the story conveys, and the old rooster acts as both a rewarder and a punisher for these two different behaviors.

What do you think of the punishment from the old rooster to the brother and sister-in-law?

A
tā men huó gāi
他们活该！
They deserve it!

B
chéng fá tài zhòng le
惩罚太重了！
The punishment is too heavy!

C
chéng fá tài qīng le
惩罚太轻了！
The punishment is too light!

D
chéng fá gōng píng
惩罚公平！
The punishment is fair!

KEY VOCABULARY

Pinyin	Chinese		English	Pinyin	Chinese		English
kě lián	可怜	*adj.*	poor (condition)	jīn	金	*n.*	gold
fù mǔ	父母	*n.*	parents	dòu zi	豆子	*n.*	bean
sǎo sao	嫂嫂	*n.*	older sister-in-law	zhí qián	值钱	*adj.*	worth money
zhòng huó	重活	*n.*	heavy work	tīng shuō	听说	*v.*	to hear
qī fù	欺负	*v.*	to bully	pāi dǎ	拍打	*v.*	to pat
gōng jī	公鸡	*n.*	rooster	dé dào	得到	*v.*	to get/obtain
pì gǔ	屁股	*n.*	butt	zhōng yú	终于	*adv.*	finally
jié guǒ	结果	*adv.*	as a result	lì kè	立刻	*adv.*	immediately

SENTENCE PATTERNS

yīn wèi ... suǒ yǐ ...
因为 ... 所以 ...

due to/because ... so ...

yīn wèi / suǒ yǐ
因为 + *reason* + **所以** + *result*

yīn wèi tā de fù mǔ sǐ le, suǒ yǐ tā hé gē ge sǎo sao zhù zài yì qǐ.
因为他的父母死了，所以他和哥哥嫂嫂住在一起。

Because his parents were dead, so he was living with his older brother and sister-in-law.

dàng ... shì ...
当 ... 是 ...

to treat/regard ... as ...

dàng / shì
A + **当** + *B* + **是** + *noun*

zhù zi dàng tā shì jiā rén.
柱子当它是家人。

Zhuzi treated it as a family member.

CHINESE VERSION

从前，有个可怜的孩子叫柱子。

因为他的父母死了，所以他和哥哥嫂嫂住在一起。

可是，他们不仅天天让他干重活，还欺负他。

后来，哥哥嫂嫂让他离开，只给了他一间破房子，一块小田和一只老公鸡。

柱子每天在田里努力干活。他对老公鸡很好，当它是家人。

一天，老公鸡突然说话，告诉柱子：

“去把我的鸡粪种在田里，能长出金豆子。”

柱子虽然很吃惊，但他照做了。

结果，几天后田里真的长满了金豆子，很值钱。

哥哥嫂嫂听说了，就去柱子的家偷了老公鸡。

他们为了得到老公鸡的鸡粪，一直拍打老公鸡的屁股。

可是，它们拍打了几天，也没有得到鸡粪。

柱子发现老公鸡不见后，非常着急，到处找老公鸡。

终于，柱子找到了哥哥嫂嫂的家，看见他们拿着刀要杀老公鸡。

柱子立刻抢过刀，救了老公鸡。

这时，老公鸡突然飞起来，在哥哥嫂嫂的脸上喷了鸡粪，然后和柱子离开了。

哥哥嫂嫂立刻去洗脸，但是洗不掉鸡粪。

而鸡粪也没变成金豆子，他们不好意思见人，从此不再出门了。

谚语故事

yàn yǔ gù shì

Chinese Proverbs

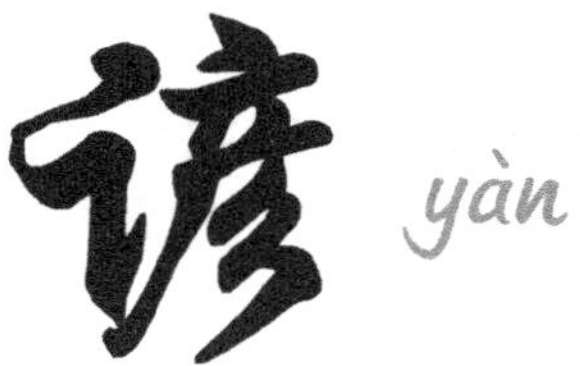

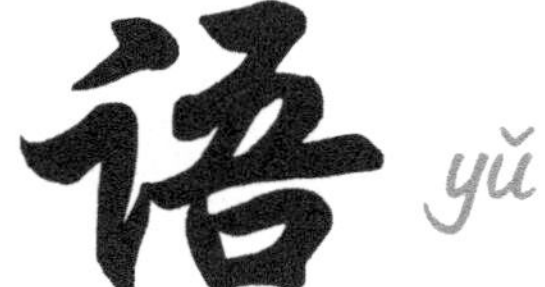

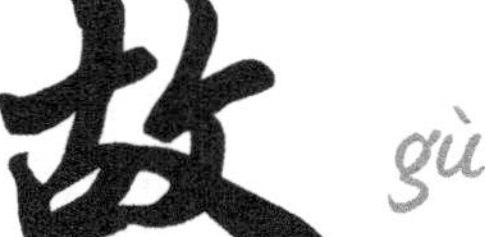

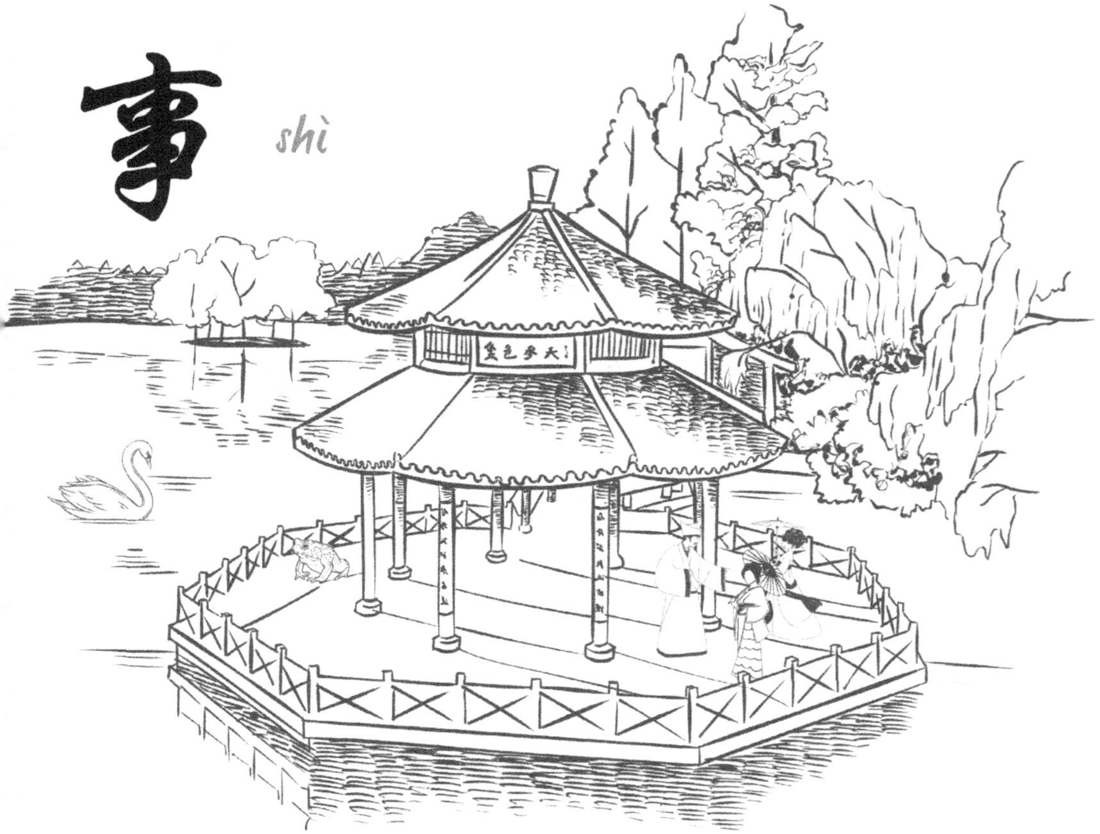

lài há ma xiǎng chī tiān é ròu

23 癞蛤蟆想吃天鹅肉

A Toad Wishing to Eat Swan Meat

yǒu gè xìng lài de yǒu qián rén zhǎng de yòu pàng yòu chǒu
有个姓赖的**有钱人**，长得又**胖**又**丑**。

There was a **rich man** with surname of Lai, he was very **fat** and **ugly**.

tā de liǎn shàng dōu shì gē da kàn shàng qù xiàng dà há ma suǒ yǐ rén men dōu jiào tā lài há ma
他的脸上都是**疙瘩**，**看上去像**大蛤蟆。所以**人们**都叫他“癞蛤蟆”。

He had **pimples** all over his face and **looked like** a big toad. Hence **people** all call him “The Favus Toad”.

lài há ma bù jǐn xǐ huān měi shí ér qiě xǐ huān měi nǚ
癞蛤蟆不仅喜欢**美食**，而且喜欢**美女**。

The Favus Toad not only liked **delicious food**, but also **beautiful women**.

tā yǒu hěn duō měi nǚ lǎo pó cháng cháng dài tā men qù dà chī dà hē
他有很多美女**老婆**，常常带她们去**大吃大喝**。

He had many beautiful women as **wives**, and often took them to **have a feast** (eat big and drink big).

yí cì tā zài jiāo wài chī fàn de shí hòu kàn dào le yí gè hěn měi de nǚ zǐ
一次，他在**郊外**吃饭的时候，看到了一个很美的**女子**。

Once, when he was eating in the **suburbs**, he saw a very beautiful **woman**.

zhè gè nǚ zi pí fū bái fēi cháng piào liàng suǒ yǐ míng zì shì bái tiān é
这个女子**皮肤**白，非常**漂亮**，所以名字是白天鹅。

This woman had fair **skin** and was very **beautiful**, so her name was Bái Tiān'é (White Swan).

lài há ma mǎ shàng qù gēn nǚ zi shuō jià wǒ ba wǒ yǒu hěn duō qián nǐ xiǎng yào shén me wǒ jiù gěi nǐ mǎi shén me
癞蛤蟆**马上**去跟女子说："**嫁**我吧，我有很多钱。你想要什么，我就给你买什么。"

The Favus Toad **immediately** went to the woman and said, "**Marry** me, I have a lot of money. I will buy you whatever you want."

bái tiān é hěn jīng yà zhè nán zi nà me chǒu tā hěn hài pà mǎ shàng jiù pǎo le
白天鹅很**惊讶**这男子**那么丑**，她很**害怕**，马上就跑了。

Bái Tiān'é was very **shocked** that the man was **so ugly**, she was **frightened**, and ran away immediately.

lài há ma bú fàng qì pài pū rén dǎ tīng bái tiān é de jiā
癞蛤蟆不**放弃**，**派**仆人**打听**白天鹅的家。

The Favus Toad did not **give up**, and **sent** servants to **inquire about** Bái Tiān'é's home.

tā mìng lìng yào shì zhǎo bu dào bái tiān é jiù huì dǎ sǐ pū rén
他命令：<u>**要是**找不到白天鹅，**就**会打死仆人。</u>

He ordered: <u>**If** Bái Tiān'é couldn't be found, he **would** beat the servant to death.</u>

hòu lái pū rén men zhōng yú zhǎo dào le bái tiān é de jiā kě shì tā yǐ jīng jié hūn le
后来，仆人们**终于**找到了白天鹅的家，可是她已经**结婚**了。

Later, the servants **finally** found Bai Tian'e's home, but she was already **married**.

lài há ma zhī dào hòu kū le tā dé le xiāng sī bìng tiān tiān jiào bái tiān é
癞蛤蟆知道后，**哭**了。他得了**相思病**，天天叫"白天鹅"。

When The Favus Toad found out, he **wept**. He became **lovesick** and cried: "Bái Tiān'é (White Swan)" every day.

hòu lái lín jū men kāi shǐ cháo xiào tā lài há ma xiǎng chī tiān é ròu
后来，**邻居们**开始**嘲笑**他：癞蛤蟆想吃天鹅肉！

Later, the **neighbors** began to **laugh at** him: "The toad wants to eat swan meat!"

Summary

This story is the origin of the proverb "癞蛤蟆想吃天鹅肉 (lài há ma xiǎng chī tiān é ròu)." The phrase itself is a bit mean and is used to joke about idiots going after the unachievable things that they don't deserve, especially refering to bad men chasing woman whom they're not worthy of. Be careful how you use this; recommended for use only for jokes or fun talks!

Learning Tip

We've all seen people we believe to be undeserving something or someone chasing after them, what examples come to your mind?

lài	há ma	xiǎng chī	tiān é	ròu
癞	蛤蟆	想吃	天鹅	肉
favus (skin disease)	toad	want to eat	swan	meat

1 yí gè bā shí suì de nán rén xiǎng qǔ yí gè shí bā suì de nǚ hái, zhēn shì lài há ma xiǎng chī tiān é ròu!

一个八十岁的男人想娶一个十八岁的女孩，**真是癞蛤蟆想吃天鹅肉！**

An eighty-year-old man wants to marry an eighteen-year-old girl, what a **toad wanting to eat swan meat**!

2 zhè gè bèn dàn xiǎng dāng zǒng tǒng, jiù xiàng lài há ma xiǎng chī tiān é ròu!

这个笨蛋想当总统，**就像癞蛤蟆想吃天鹅肉！**

This idiot wants to be president, just like a **toad wants to eat a swan meat**!

Write your own sentence

Key vocabulary

pàng 胖	*adj.*	fat	piào liàng 漂亮	*adj.*	beautiful
chǒu 丑	*adj.*	ugly	pí fū 皮肤	n.	skin
měi shí 美食	*n.*	delicious food	jīng yà 惊讶	*adj.*	shocked
měi nǚ 美女	*n.*	beautiful woman	hài pà 害怕	*v.*	to be frightened
lǎo pó 老婆	*n.*	wife	fàng qì 放弃	*v.*	to give up
lǎo gōng 老公	*n.*	husband	dǎ tīng 打听	*v.*	to enquire about
dà chī dà hē 大吃大喝	*vp.*	have a feast	xiāng sī bìng 相思病	*n.*	lovesickness
tiān é 天鹅	*n.*	swan	há ma 蛤蟆	*n.*	toad
jià 嫁	*v.*	to marry (woman to man)	cháo xiào 嘲笑	*v.*	to mock/ laugh at

Sentence patterns

kàn shàng qù xiàng
看上去像 ...

looks like ...

subject + **看上去像** (kàn shàng qù xiàng) + *noun*

tā kàn shàng qù xiàng dà há ma
他看上去像大蛤蟆。

He looked like a big toad.

yào shì ... jiù
要是 ... 就 ...

to form a conditional statement

要是 (yào shì) + *condition* + **就** (jiù) + *result*

tā mìng lìng : yào shì zhǎo bù dào bái tiān é, jiù huì dǎ sǐ pū rén
他命令：要是找不到白天鹅，就会打死仆人。

He ordered: If Bái Tiān'é couldn't be found, he would beat the servant to death.

CHINESE VERSION

有个姓赖的有钱人，长得又胖又丑。

他的脸上都是疙瘩，看上去像大蛤蟆。所以人们都叫他"癞蛤蟆"

癞蛤蟆不仅喜欢美食，而且喜欢美女。

他有很多美女老婆，常常带她们去大吃大喝。

一次，他在郊外吃饭的时候，看到了一个很美的女子。

这个女子皮肤白，非常漂亮，所以名字是白天鹅。

癞蛤蟆马上去跟女子说："嫁我吧，我有很多钱。你想要什么，我就给你买什么。"

白天鹅很惊讶这男子那么丑，她很害怕，马上就跑了。

癞蛤蟆不放弃，派仆人打听白天鹅的家。

他命令：要是找不到白天鹅，就会打死仆人。

后来，仆人们终于找到了白天鹅的家，可是她已经结婚了。

癞蛤蟆知道后，哭了。他得了相思病，天天叫"白天鹅"。

后来，邻居们开始嘲笑他：癞蛤蟆想吃天鹅肉！

jìn zhū zhě chì jìn mò zhě hēi

近朱者赤，近墨者黑 24

One Takes the Behavior of One's Company

zài jìn cháo yǒu yí gè pǐn xué jiān yōu de xué zhě jiào bó xuán
在晋朝，有一个**品学兼优**的学者叫博玄。

In the Jin Dynasty, there was a scholar named Bo Xuan who was **excellent in both character and study**.

yīn wèi bó xuán shì zhèng fǔ de yì míng zhèng pài guān yuán suǒ yǐ huáng dì fēi cháng zūn jìng tā
因为博玄是政府的一名**正派**官员，所以皇帝非常**尊敬**他。

Because Bo Xuan was an **upright** official of the government, the emperor **respected** him very much.

hòu lái wèi le bāng zhù jiào yù tài zi huáng dì jiù qǐng bó xuán dāng tài zi de lǎo shī
后来，为了帮助**教育**太子，皇帝就**请**博玄**当**太子的老师。

Later, in order to help **educate** the crown prince, the emperor **asked** Bo Xuan **to be** the prince's teacher.

bó xuán dào le tài zi de gōng diàn hòu fā xiàn tài zi fēi cháng tān wán tǎo yàn xué xí
博玄到了太子的**宫殿**后，发现太子非常**贪玩**，**讨厌**学习。

After Bo Xuan arrived at the prince's **palace**, he found that the prince was very **playful** and **disliked** learning.

yú shì bó xuán jiù zǐ xì guān chá le tài zi zhōu biān de péng yǒu hé pū rén
于是，博玄就仔细**观察**了太子**周边**的朋友和仆人。

So, Bo Xuan carefully **observed** the friends and servants **around** the prince.

tā fā xiàn zhè xiē rén yào me tān wán yào me lǎn duò
他发现，这些人**要么**贪玩，**要么**懒惰。

He found that these people were **either** playful **or** lazy.

ér qiě dà jiā dōu zhǐ xiǎng tǎo hǎo tài zi zǒng shì gǔ lì tā duō wán
而且，大家都只想**讨好**太子，总是**鼓励**他多玩。

Moreover, everyone just wanted **to please** the prince and always **encouraged** him to play more.

yú shì bó xuán jiě gù le tā men rán hòu tā huàn shàng le yì xiē pǐn xué jiān yōu de xīn rén
于是，博玄**解雇**了他们。然后，他换上了一些**品学兼优**的新人。

So Bo Xuan **dismissed** them. Then, he replaced them with some newcomers with **excellent character and study**.

tài zi suī rán hěn shēng qì dàn shì méi yǒu fǎn kàng
太子虽然很**生气**，但是没有**反抗**。

Although the prince was very **angry**, he did not **resist**.

màn màn de tài zi kāi shǐ hé zhōu wéi de xīn rén jiāo péng yǒu
慢慢地，太子开始**和**周围的新人**交朋友**。

Gradually, the prince began **to make friends with** the new people around him.

jiē zhe tā shòu tā men de yǐng xiǎng zài xué xí shàng biàn rèn zhēn le
接着，他受他们的**影响**，在学习上变**认真**了。

Then, under their **influence**, he became **serious** about his studies.

huáng dì zhī dào hòu fēi cháng gāo xìng jiù wèn bó xuán wéi shén me huì yòng zhè gè fāng fǎ
皇帝知道后非常高兴，就问博玄**为什么**会用这个**方法**。

The emperor was very happy when he heard out, and asked Bo Xuan **why** he used this **method**.

bó xuán huí dá jìn zhū zhě chì jìn mò zhě hēi
博玄**回答**：近朱者赤，近墨者黑。

Bo Xuan **replied**: "One takes the behavior of one's company (Those who are close to vermilion become red, those who are close to ink become black)."

zhǐ yǒu ràng tài zi zhōu wéi duō yì xiē zhèng pài de rén, tā cái huì xué hǎo
只有让太子周围多一些正派的人，他**才**会学好。

Only when the prince is surrounded by more upright people, he would **then** learn to be good.

fǎn zhī, tā hěn kě néng huì xué huài
反之，他很可能会学坏。

Conversely, he is likely to learn to be bad (when the opposite is true).

huáng dì tīng hòu, jué de fēi cháng zhèng què, jiù qǐng rén xiě xià le zhè jù huà
皇帝听后，觉得非常**正确**，就请人**写下**了这句话，

After the emperor heard this, he felt it was very **correct**, so he asked someone to **write down** this sentence,

rán hòu pài rén bǎ tā guà zài tài zi de shū fáng, ràng tài zi tiān tiān lǎng dú
然后**派**人把它挂在太子的**书房**，让太子天天**朗读**。

then he **sent** someone to hang it in the prince's **study room** and asked the prince **read** it **aloud** every day.

SUMMARY

This story is the origin of the proverb "近朱者赤，近墨者黑." This proverb means that if we are close to good people, we will likely be good; but if we are close to bad people, we will likely be bad. Indicating that our behaviors can be easily influenced by people surrounding us! This proverb is used to emphasize this point and encourages us to connect and associate with people who are good and have positive influences.

Learning Tip

Just as the paint from a brush always manages to somehow end up on your clothes when painting a room, the behaviour of those we closely associate with rubs off on us. Can you think of a time this has been true in your experience?

jìn	zhū	zhě	chì	jìn	mò	zhě	hēi
近	朱	者	赤	近	墨	者	黑
close	vermilion	person	red	close	ink	person	black

1 jìn zhū zhě chì, jìn mò zhě hēi. bù yào gēn liú máng lái wǎng.
近朱者赤，近墨者黑。不要跟流氓来往。
One takes the behavior of one's company. Don't hang out with gangsters.

2 jìn zhū zhě chì, jìn mò zhě hēi. nǐ xiǎng biàn de yōu xiù, jiù hé yōu xiù de rén lái wǎng.
近朱者赤，近墨者黑。你想变得优秀，就和优秀的人来往。
One takes the behavior of one's company. If you want to be excellent, hang out with excellent people.

Write your own sentence

Key vocabulary

zhèng pài 正派	*adj.*	upright	tǎo hǎo 讨好	*v.*	to please
zūn jìng 尊敬	*v.*	to respect	gǔ lì 鼓励	v.	to encourage
jiào yù 教育	*v.*	to educate	jiě gù 解雇	*v.*	to dismiss
gōng diàn 宫殿	*n.*	palace	zhèng fǔ 政府	*n.*	government
tān wán 贪玩	*adj.*	playful	fǎn kàng 反抗	*v.*	to resist
tǎo yàn 讨厌	*v.* *adj.*	to dislike annoying	rèn zhēn 认真	*adj.*	serious (attitude)
guān chá 观察	*v.*	to observe	fāng fǎ 方法	*n.*	method
zhōu wéi 周围	*n.*	surrounding	fǎn zhī 反之	*conj.*	conversely
pǐn xué jiān yōu 品学兼优	*idiom*	excellent in character and study	zhèng què 正确	*adj.*	correct

Sentence patterns

hé jiāo péng yǒu 和 ... 交朋友

make friends with

A + **hé 和** + *B* + **jiāo péng yǒu 交朋友**

tài zi kāi shǐ hé xīn rén jiāo péng yǒu
太子开始和新人交朋友。

The prince began to make friends with the new people.

zhǐ yǒu cái 只有 ... 才 ...

only by ... (then) ...

zhǐ yǒu 只有 + *condition* + **cái 才** + *result*

zhǐ yǒu ràng tài zi zhōu wéi duō yì xiē zhèng pài de rén, tā cái huì xué hǎo
只有让太子周围多一些正派的人，他才会学好。

Only when the prince is surrounded by more upright people, he would then learn to be good.

CHINESE VERSION

在晋朝,有一个品学兼优的学者叫博玄。

因为博玄是政府的一名正派官员,所以皇帝非常尊敬他。

后来,为了帮助教育太子,皇帝就请博玄当太子的老师。

博玄到了太子的宫殿后,发现太子非常贪玩,讨厌学习。

于是,博玄就仔细观察了太子周边的朋友和仆人。

他发现,这些人要么贪玩,要么懒惰。

而且,大家都只想讨好太子,总是鼓励他多玩。

于是,博玄解雇了他们。

然后,他换上了一些品学兼优的新人。

太子虽然很生气,但是没有反抗。

慢慢地,太子开始和周围的新人交朋友。

接着,他受他们的影响,在学习上变认真了。

皇帝知道后非常高兴,就问博玄为什么会用这个方法。

博玄回答:近朱者赤,近墨者黑。

只有让太子周围多一些正派的人,他才会学好。

反之,他很可能会学坏。

皇帝听后,觉得非常正确,就请人写下了这句话,

然后派人把它挂在太子的书房,让太子天天朗读。

hǎo shì bù chū mén huài shì chuán qiān lǐ

好事不出门，坏事传千里

Good News Goes on Crutches, Bad News Travels Fast

jìn cháo de yí wèi shǒu xiàng hé níng tā nián qīng de shí hòu hěn shuài yǒu hěn duō nǚ péng yǒu

晋朝的一位**首相**和凝，他**年轻**的时候，很**帅**，有很多**女朋友**。

There was a **prime minister** in the Jin Dynasty called He Ning. When he was **young**, he was very **handsome**, and had many **girlfriends**.

tā xiě le hěn duō qíng gē dōu shì guān yú yǔ měi rén huò zhě jì nǚ yuē huì

他写了很多**情歌**，都是**关于**与美人或者**妓女**约会。

He wrote a lot of **love songs**, often **about** dating beauties or **prostitutes**.

yīn wèi tā de qíng gē hěn chū míng suǒ yǐ hěn duō rén dōu rèn shi tā

因为他的情歌很**出名**，所以很多人都**认识**他。

Because his love songs are very **famous**, so many people **know** him.

hěn duō nián hòu tā jīng guò nǔ lì dāng shàng le shǒu xiàng

很多年后，他**经过**努力**当上**了首相。

Years later, **after** working hard, he **became** the prime minister.

kě shì tā hěn dān xīn nà xiē qíng gē huì duì tā yǒu huài yǐng xiǎng

可是，他很担心那些情歌会**对**他有坏**影响**。

However, he was very worried that those love songs would **have** a bad **impact on** him.

yú shì, tā xiān pài rén shōu jí le nà xiē qíng gē, rán hòu bǎ tā men shāo le。
于是，他**先**派人收集了那些情歌，**然后**把它们烧了。

So, he **first** sent people to collect those love songs, **then** he burned them.

hé níng qí shí shì yí gè hǎo guān, cháng cháng wèi guó jiā hé rén mín zuò hǎo shì。
和凝**其实**是一个好官，常常为**国家**和**人民**做好事。

He Ning was **actually** a good official, often doing good deeds for the **country** and the **people**.

yí cì, hé níng pài dà shǐ qù wài guó bài fǎng。
一次，和凝派**大使**去外国**拜访**。

Once, He Ning sent an **ambassador** to a foreign country to **visit**.

dà shǐ dào hòu, jiāo ào de shuō: "wǒ shì wǒ guó shǒu xiàng pài lái de。"
大使到后，**骄傲**地说："我是我国**首相**派来的。"

After the ambassador arrived, he **proudly** said: "I was sent by our **prime minister**."

wài guó de dài biǎo jiù cháo xiào tā shuō: "ó, jiù shì nà gè xiě qíng gē de rén!"
外国的**代表**就嘲笑他说："哦，就是那个写**情歌**的人！"

The foreign **representatives** laughed at him and said, "Oh, the one who wrote **love songs**!"

dà shǐ fēi cháng bù hǎo yì si, hòu lái gào sù le hé níng zhè jiàn shì。
大使非常**不好意思**，后来**告诉**了和凝这件事。

The ambassador was very **embarrassed**, and later **told** He Ning about it.

hé níng tàn qì, shuō: "hǎo shì bù chū mén, huài shì chuán qiān lǐ。 dà jiā zhǐ jì dé wǒ de huài shì a!"
和凝**叹气**，说："好事不出门，坏事传千里。大家只**记得**我的坏事啊！"

He Ning **sighed** and said: "Good news goes on crutches, bad news travels fast. People only **remember** my bad things!"

hòu lái, zhè jiàn shì jiù chuán kāi le, zhè jù huà yě chéng le jīng diǎn。
后来，这件事就**传开**了，这句话也成了**经典**。

Later, this incident **spread**, and this sentence has also become a **classic**.

Summary

This story is the origin of the proverb "好事不出门，坏事传千." The proverb means that bad news always travels faster than good news, as bad news tends to draw more attention than good news! Even in modern days, often it is the bad news that catches the **headlines** (头条)! The proverb is used to emphasize this and encourages us to do more good than bad.

Learning Tip

Can you think of some example of where this proverb has proved true in your experience?

hǎo shì	bù	chū mén	huài shì	chuán	qiān lǐ
好事	不	出门	坏事	传	千里
good things	no	go out	bad things	spread	thousand miles

1 tā de chǒu wén shàng tóu tiáo le ! zhēn shì : hǎo shì bù chū mén, huài shì chuán qiān lǐ !
他的丑闻上头条了！真是：好事不出门，坏事传千里！

His scandal hit the headlines! Really is: **Good news goes on crutches, bad news travels fast!**

2 bù néng gào sù bié rén, yào jì zhù : hǎo shì bù chū mén, huài shì chuán qiān lǐ !
不能告诉别人，要记住：好事不出门，坏事传千里！

Don't tell others, remember: **Good news goes on crutches, bad news travels fast!**

Write your own sentence

Key vocabulary

shǒu xiàng 首相	*n.*	prime minister	qí shí 其实	*adv.*	actually
yuē huì 约会	*v.*	to date	dà shǐ 大使	n.	ambassador
shuài 帅	*adj.*	handsome	bài fǎng 拜访	*v.*	to visit (formal)
qíng gē 情歌	*n.*	love song	jiāo ào 骄傲	*adj.*	proud
guān yú 关于	*pre.*	about	dài biǎo 代表	*n.*	representative
jì nǚ 妓女	*n.*	prostitute	bù hǎo yì si 不好意思	*adj.*	embarrassed
chū míng 出名	*adj.*	famous	tàn qì 叹气	*v.*	to sign
dāng shàng 当上	*v.*	to become (new job role)	chuán kāi 传开	*v.*	to spread
yǐng xiǎng 影响	*n.* *v.*	effect to affect	jīng diǎn 经典	*n.*	classic

Sentence patterns

duì yǒu yǐng xiǎng 对 … 有影响

has influence/impact on

duì yǒu yǐng xiǎng
A + **对** + *B* + **有影响**

tā hěn dān xīn nà xiē qíng gē huì duì tā yǒu huài yǐng xiǎng
他很担心那些情歌会对他有坏影响。

He worried that those love songs would have a bad impact on him.

xiān rán hòu 先 … 然后

first … then …

xiān rán hòu
先 + *action 1* + **然后** + *action 2*

tā xiān pài rén shōu jí le nà xiē qíng gē, rán hòu bǎ tā men shāo le
他先派人收集了那些情歌，然后把它们烧了。

He first sent people to collect those love songs, then he burned them.

CHINESE VERSION

晋朝的一位首相和凝，他年轻的时候，很帅，有很多女朋友。

他写了很多情歌，都是关于与美人或者妓女约会。

因为他的情歌很出名，所以很多人都认识他。

很多年后，他经过努力当上了首相。

可是，他很担心那些情歌会对他有坏影响。

于是，他先派人收集了那些情歌，然后把它们烧了。

和凝其实是一个好官，常常为国家和人民做好事。

一次，和凝派大使去外国拜访。

大使到后，骄傲地说："我是我国首相派来的。"

外国的代表就嘲笑他说："哦，就是那个写情歌的人！"

大使非常不好意思，后来告诉了和凝这件事。

和凝叹气，说："好事不出门，坏事传千里"。大家只记得我的坏事啊！"

后来，这件事就传开了，这句话也成了经典。

ACCESS AUDIO

I highly encourage you to use the accompanying audio recordings for all of the examples in this book, not only will it help to improve your listening skills but if you are unfamiliar or unsure about the pronunciations of any words in this book, then you can listen to them spoken by native speakers.

Instructions to Access Audio

1. **Scan this QR code** →
   or go to: **www.linglingmandarin.com/books**

2. Locate this book in the list of LingLing Mandarin Books

3. Click the "Access Audio" button   Access Audio

4. Enter the password:

THE NEXT STAGE

Congratulations on reaching the end of this book! By now, you're well on your way to progressing to the intermediate level. It is my pleasure to welcome you to the next stage with my second book of my Chinese Story Series: **Chinese Stories for Language Learners: Intermediate**, featuring:

- Over 30 new exciting stories from Chinese myths, fables, idioms, proverbs, and famous modern and historical figures.
- Inspiring stories of influential figures like Jack Ma and Bruce Lee.
- Legendary characters from Ancient China like Wu Zetian (*the first and only empress of China*) and Qu Yuan (*the founder of Chinese romanticism*).
- Iconic periods and people of Chinese history
- Intriguing and colorful characters and stories from the renowned Romance of the Three Kingdoms.
- Accelerate your progress toward fluency. Master more vocabulary, sentence patterns, idioms, and proverbs for everyday speech.

Available now:
https://amzn.to/3IQ10Cf

GET YOUR FREE EBOOK NOW

linglingmandarin.com/beginner-bundle

BOOKS BY LINGLING

CHINESE CONVERSATIONS
FOR BEGINNERS

CHINESE CONVERSATIONS
FOR INTERMEDIATE

MANDARIN WRITING
PRACTICE BOOK

CHINESE STORIES FOR
LANGUAGE LEARNERS:
ELEMENTARY

CHINESE STORIES FOR
LANGUAGE LEARNERS:
INTERMEDIATE

THE ART OF WAR
FOR LANGUAGE
LEARNERS

Get notified about **new releases**
https://linglingmandarin.com/notify

NEW HSK VOCABULARY SERIES

LEARN CHINESE VOCABULARY FOR BEGINNERS:
NEW HSK 1

LEARN CHINESE VOCABULARY FOR BEGINNERS:
NEW HSK 2

LEARN CHINESE VOCABULARY FOR BEGINNERS:
NEW HSK 3

LEARN CHINESE VOCABULARY FOR INTERMEDIATE:
NEW HSK 4

LEARN CHINESE VOCABULARY FOR INTERMEDIATE:
NEW HSK 5

LEARN CHINESE VOCABULARY FOR INTERMEDIATE:
NEW HSK 6

Get notified about **new releases**
https://linglingmandarin.com/notify

ABOUT THE AUTHOR

LingLing is a native Chinese Mandarin educator with an MA in Communication and Language. Originally from China, now living in the UK, she is the founder of the learning brand LingLing Mandarin, which aims to create the best resources for learners to master the Chinese language and achieve deep insight into Chinese culture in a fun and illuminating way. Discover more about LingLing and access more great resources by following the links below or scanning the QR codes.

WEBSITE

linglingmandarin.com

YOUTUBE CHANNEL

youtube.com/c/linglingmandarin

PATREON

patreon.com/linglingmandarin

INSTAGRAM

instagram.com/linglingmandarin

Made in the USA
Las Vegas, NV
09 April 2024

88437453R00090